THE
PERSONAL
ACCOUNTABILITY
CODE™

The Step-by-Step Guide to a Winning Strategy that Transforms Your Goals into Reality with the *New* Science of Accountability

DI WORRALL

The Personal Accountability Code™
© 2014 Di Worrall
A publication of

THE ACCOUNTABILITY CODE™

All Rights Reserved. This book may not be reproduced or transmitted in whole or in part, by any means, without written consent of the author or publisher—with the exception of the purchaser for their personal use, and reviewers who may quote brief passages. Outside of this usage, requests for permission should be directed to **enquiry@worrallassociates.com.au**, or mailed to Worrall & Associates, PO Box 4041, Carlton NSW Australia, 2218.

The information, advice and strategies presented herein represent the views of the author at the date of publication. Due to the rate at which conditions change, the author reserves the right to alter and update her opinions at any time. While every attempt has been made to verify the information and strategies in this book, the author does not assume any responsibility for errors, inaccuracies or omissions. The advice and strategies contained herein may not be applicable to every situation. If professional assistance is required, then the services of a qualified professional should be sought.

First Edition: December 2014

Cover Design & Interior Layout Artists: Adina Cucicov Flamingo Design
Consulting Editor: Patsi Krakoff www.contentforcoaches.com
Copy Editor and Proofreader: Debbie Brunettin
Curriculum Designer: Kathy Green
Technology Consultants: Tim Williams www.awebsitethatworksforyou.com.au
Graphic Designer: Ilija Visnjic

TABLE OF CONTENTS

Preface: A Message from the Author 1

Introduction 5
    Why Have a Plan? 5
    Why Do Most Plans Fail? 5
    Why Traditional Goal Setting Sets Us Up for Failure 6
    Introducing the New Science of Accountability 7
    Who is This Guide for? 8
    How to Use This Guide 8
    Objectives for Each Chapter 9
    Chapter Summaries 11
    Three Editions to Choose From 16
    How to Use This Guide 16
    Upgrading to The Personal Accountability Code™ (Premium) Edition 17

Step 1: Are You Ready for Change? 19
    Purpose of This Chapter 20
    Are You Ready for Change? 20
    Responsibility vs. Accountability 21
    Do You Really *Want* to Change? 22
    How Ready Are You for Responsibility? 23
    The Responsibility-Readiness Assessment 25
    The Secrets of Highly Successful (and Accountable) People 30
    Holding High-Accountability Conversations 31
    Personal Accountability Index 32
    How to Work on Your 'Accountability Ability' 36

Accountability Partnerships	36
Why Engage a Career or Life Coach?	42
What a coach doesn't do	42
It's the Small Wins That Count	44

Step 2: Where Are You Going? — 47

Purpose of This Chapter	48
Crystallise Your Purpose by Crafting Your Vision of the Future	48
The Visioning Tool	50
Tell Your Story	50
The Values Exercise	52
My Values	55
Prioritising My Values	56

Step 3: Who Are You? — 59

Purpose of This Chapter	60
Optimising Your Environment—What Drives You?	61
Optimising Your Environment—The Work Styles Self-Assessment	64
Optimising Your Environment—What Motivates You?	71
Optimising Your Environment—Know Your Strengths	72
The Truth About Self-Discipline	74
Know How to Ask for Feedback	75
The Feedforward Exercise	76

Step 4: Where Are You Now? — 79

Purpose of This Chapter	80
The Wheel of Life	81
SPOT Analysis	86
Strengths	87
Problems	88
Gap Analysis	90
Opportunities (in Your Environment)	92
Threats (in Your Environment)	93
The Truth About Habits	94

Step 5: How Are You Getting There? 101
   Purpose of This Chapter 102
   Why Set Goals? 103
   Benefits of Goal Setting 104
   Characteristics of Effective Goals 104
   A Process for Successful Goal Achievement 105
   Goal Achievement Step 1—Select Specific Goals 106
   Goal Achievement Step 2—Measure Success 112
   Goal Achievement Step 3—Determine Action Steps 114
   Goal Achievement Step 4—Be Realistic 117
   Goal Achievement Step 5—Align to a Timeframe 118

Step 6: How Will You Stay on Track? 121
   Purpose of This Chapter 122
   Goal Achievement Step 6—Ensure Goals are Energising 124
   Goal Achievement Step 7—Reinforce Progress 125
   Winning with Personal Accountability & Goals 130

The Accountability Coach 133
   1. Getting Back on Track After a Setback 134
   2. How to Hold Others Accountable 137
   4. How to be Motivated When Goals Have Been Imposed Upon You 148
   5. 10 of the Best Tips for Overcoming Procrastination 151
   6. How to Focus on Goals When ____ Gets in the Way 154

Appendix 1: Do's and Don'ts of Winning with The Personal Accountability Code™ 157
Appendix 2: My Accountability Action Plan 159
Di Worrall 165
Other Books from Di Worrall 169

PREFACE

A Message from the Author

Congratulations on your decision to take the reins of your life. It's a decision that may be one of the most important you ever make.

The Personal Accountability Code™ was born of the concepts first introduced in my #1 Amazon bestseller *Accountability Leadership*. If you have arrived at this Guide by finding something in *Accountability Leadership* that whet your appetite for more, then you are in for a treat. In *The Personal Accountability Code*™, we take the power of positive accountability and bring you a pragmatic 'how-to' guide for people who want more success designing and fulfilling the life and career that works for them. Not just leaders—but anyone who is committed to making positive, sustainable change in their life or career.

In my experience, successful goal achievers share an undeniable truth: they are winners in the business of goal achievement, because they have adopted the *new* science of positive principled accountability and responsibility. As you make your way through the six modules of *The Personal Accountability Code*™, you will not only have the opportunity to develop the same winning strategies for personal change that successful goal achievers use, but you will also create powerful systems of tracking your progress and staying motivated that will see you through in the face of inevitable setbacks.

THE PERSONAL ACCOUNTABILITY CODE™

Setback and failure are nothing to shy away from. In fact, the more spectacular the failure, the more it is likely to be amongst our most defining moments in life—depending on how we choose to handle it. We can choose to accept our role in creating the outcome, and appreciate the opportunity for the learning and growth it represents (even accepting our role in hindsight works). Or we can choose to suffer and waste our energy under the weight of guilt, self-consciousness and deflected blame. By choosing the path of personal accountability, we can make it through life's 'moments' with greater self-esteem, as a better person or better professional with more strength and wisdom to give back to the world and rise to our next personal challenge.

Why is accountability and responsibility the key platform for successful change in *The Personal Accountability Code*™? Poor systems and skills in accountability and responsibility are the fundamental cause of failure in business and life, and yet they are amongst the least-addressed competencies. Worse still, poor personal accountability is a leading cause of chronic stress. Failure to take adequate responsibility and accountability are so insidiously interwoven into the fabric of our modern lifestyle that they are nearly invisible, and the costs to our health, well-being and success can be high.

In this Guide, *The Personal Accountability Code*™ has been distilled into a six-step process designed to help individuals unravel these blind spots and eliminate the consequences of poor accountability, revealing a new path for successful change. By completing the exercises in this Guide, you will create your own winning strategy for transforming your goals and intentions into reality while building your accountability and responsibility muscles seamlessly along your journey of personal transformation.

The *new* science of accountability has revolutionised the way we see accountability and responsibility. The traditional perspective of accountability and responsibility is weighed down with the stigma of negativity through punitive measures of control and punishment. Sadly, we all too often connect accountability to *the pointing finger*, which waits, conspiring to catch us out and apportion blame as soon as something goes wrong.

The new science of accountability and responsibility is a vastly different paradigm; a virtually untapped goldmine of positive principled growth, motivation and reward. With the new skills you will develop in *The Personal Accountability Code*™, you will connect to your natural energy reserves, drive and enthusiasm, and finally pave a clear pathway for designing and fulfilling the life and career you've dreamed of.

Let's Begin.

Your Coach,
DI WORRALL

The Personal Accountability Code

The Personal Accountability Code™

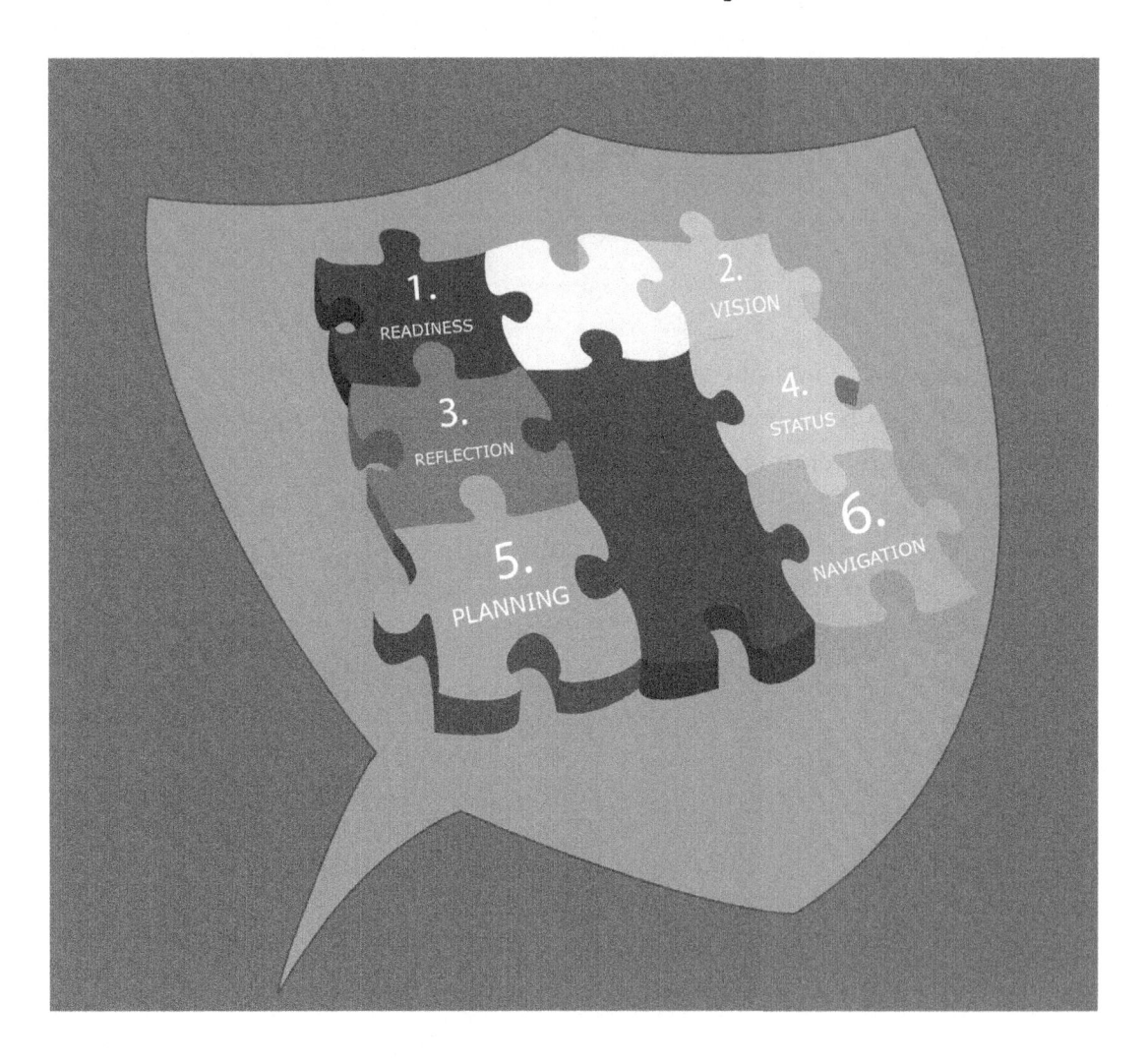

1. READINESS
2. VISION
3. REFLECTION
4. STATUS
5. PLANNING
6. NAVIGATION

INTRODUCTION

Why Have a Plan?

> *'If you don't design your own life plan, chances are you'll fall into someone else's plan. And guess what they have planned for you? Not much.'*
>
> **Jim Rohn**

The Personal Accountability Code™ takes you step-by-step through the powerful process of creating the life or career you desire and deserve.

You may have heard that writing down your plans and intentions is a very powerful action. It is. But it doesn't stop there.

Even more powerful is your capacity to follow through on your good intentions—especially when setbacks occur. Even for the most successful amongst us, one thing can be guaranteed: setbacks will inevitably happen with any worthwhile effort to make change. What differentiates those who make it from those who don't is how you pick yourself up again when things don't go according to plan.

Why Do Most Plans Fail?

The corporate world can cite many a story of business plans that failed to deliver on their original intentions. It is recognised that such failures more frequently occur not in the planning but in the execution and follow-up. The pages of the corporate manual of good intentions are littered with great plans that bit the dust as just another victim to poor systems of accountability.

What you don't often hear is that the same is true for most *personal* failure. It's all too easy to find plenty of excuses to abandon our intentions for change and revert to our comfortable old ways when things get tough. We are masters of maintaining the status quo. Our subconscious is the king of trickery—whispering in our ear that the 'known' is safe and the 'known' can be trusted. So our subconscious can really only reach one conclusion about the 'unknown': no matter how enticing it may look in the distance, the unknown cannot be trusted, is not safe and holds hidden dangers.

With this internal battle in play each time we strive to make life changes, it's no wonder that few people achieve the goals they truly want. When something goes wrong, we raise our barriers of resistance to change and choose to be unaccountable to our own intentions in order to keep safe and remain sane.

We even do this at the expense of our own health and happiness. Weird, isn't it?

Why Traditional Goal Setting Sets Us Up for Failure

We set ourselves up to fail if we continue to surround ourselves with inadequate, negative or uninspiring systems or people that divert us from the path to our dreams and goals.

It's not as though we set out to fail. Failure is rarely deliberate. You've probably heard the old saying, 'Trying to make a silk purse out of a sow's ear.' Well, in this context, the old methods of staying on track no longer work when it comes to inspiring and motivating us to stay true to our intentions (if they ever did). The old ways of goal achievement set us up to fail because:

- We head off ill-prepared for stepping up to the changes in accountability and responsibility we will face
- We frequently pursue a vision which is not our own and which does not align with our highest personal values
- Traditional methods of goal selection exhaust the limits of our willpower as they rarely align with our greatest natural sources of inner strength, inspiration, energy and motivation

Introduction

- The old methods of keeping on track are rife with built-in excuses that encourage us to see it as okay if we bail out early rather than risk failure. We sidestep greater personal responsibility, avoid pursuing challenging goals, or give up because the challenge is just too far out of our comfort zone
- The old methods of goal planning cause us to *bite off more than we can chew. Failure to focus on our highest priorities leaves us with too many to-dos, so we don't*
- The old ways fail to adequately plan for and stock up the necessary resources to address the obstacles that inevitably lie ahead
- The old ways see us gravitate towards people who let us off the hook and buy into our excuses

The Personal Accountability Code™ disrupts this pattern of systemic failure in personal accountability through the *new* science of accountability.

Introducing the New Science of Accountability

As you would expect, the approach used in this Guide to designing a new path for your life and work goals addresses all of the exciting, shiny new things you would expect to see in such a resource for goal setting and personal achievement. However, unlike many other resources, this Guide also partners with you to face head-on the often neglected area of goal failure (before it happens). Woven throughout each of the six modules is the positive, principled and energising *new* science of accountability, from your vision through to goal completion, follow-through and motivation when times get tough.

As you complete the exercises in each chapter, you will progressively create a simple yet <u>consistent</u> strategy for building your own *Personal Accountability Code*™ and the capacity to finally stay accountable to your life and work goals by:

- Tapping into and unleashing the many sources of drive, energy, strength and motivation that are naturally available to you
- Ensuring your intentions for change are aligned with your highest life values
- Navigating a clear path from your vision for change right through to successful goal fulfilment

The Personal Accountability Code

- Building a cadre of motivational, reinforcing systems that serve as your own personal coach and cheer squad to congratulate you when things go right and pick you up when things go wrong
- Ensuring you are ready for the changes ahead by building your responsibility and accountability muscles
- Being prepared for the inevitable bumps in the road by doing a reality check on the traits, resources and skills you do and don't have available to you, so you can gather what you need *before* you begin your journey
- Growing your confidence and transforming your competence to achieve what you really want in life and at work

Who is This Guide for?

The Personal Accountability Code™ is for anyone who is committed to personal or professional change. This includes:

- Individuals who are stepping up to take the leadership reins of their own lives in pursuit of personal or professional development goals
- Professionals who are in the business of coaching others in their career and life goals; e.g., life coaches and career coaches

How to Use This Guide

This Guide outlines a six-step process for creating a winning strategy for transforming your intentions into reality that will break through the barriers which typically hold people back from achieving their goals. Each process of *The Accountability Code*™ is captured in a powerful question that will challenge, inspire and uplift you on your quest to design and succeed in creating the life of your dreams.

  Step 1: Are You Ready for Change?

  Step 2: Where Are You Going?

  Step 3: Who Are You?

  Step 4: Where Are You Now?

Step 5: How Are You Getting There?

Step 6: How Will You Stay on Track?

You will have the opportunity, through this Guide, to explore each of these questions in detail by working through the exercises in their corresponding chapter. By the end of the Guide, you will have unravelled your own *Personal Accountability Code*™ and created a winning strategy for personal change that is unique to you and built into your Personal Accountability Plan and Follow-Up System.

Objectives for Each Chapter

1. **Context:** To understand the context of the chapter and how the new science of accountability is critical to successful goal achievement
2. **Exercises:** To complete personal worksheet exercises that gather the background information and self-analysis required to complete a key component of your *Personal Accountability Code*™
3. **Accountability Plan:** To prepare a key component of your Personal Accountability Action Plan
4. **Accountability System:** To prepare a key component of your Personal Accountability Follow-Up System

THE **6** Step Process for Winning with **The Personal Accountability Code** ™

From Winning Strategy To Lasting Reality
The Journey of Personal Transformation

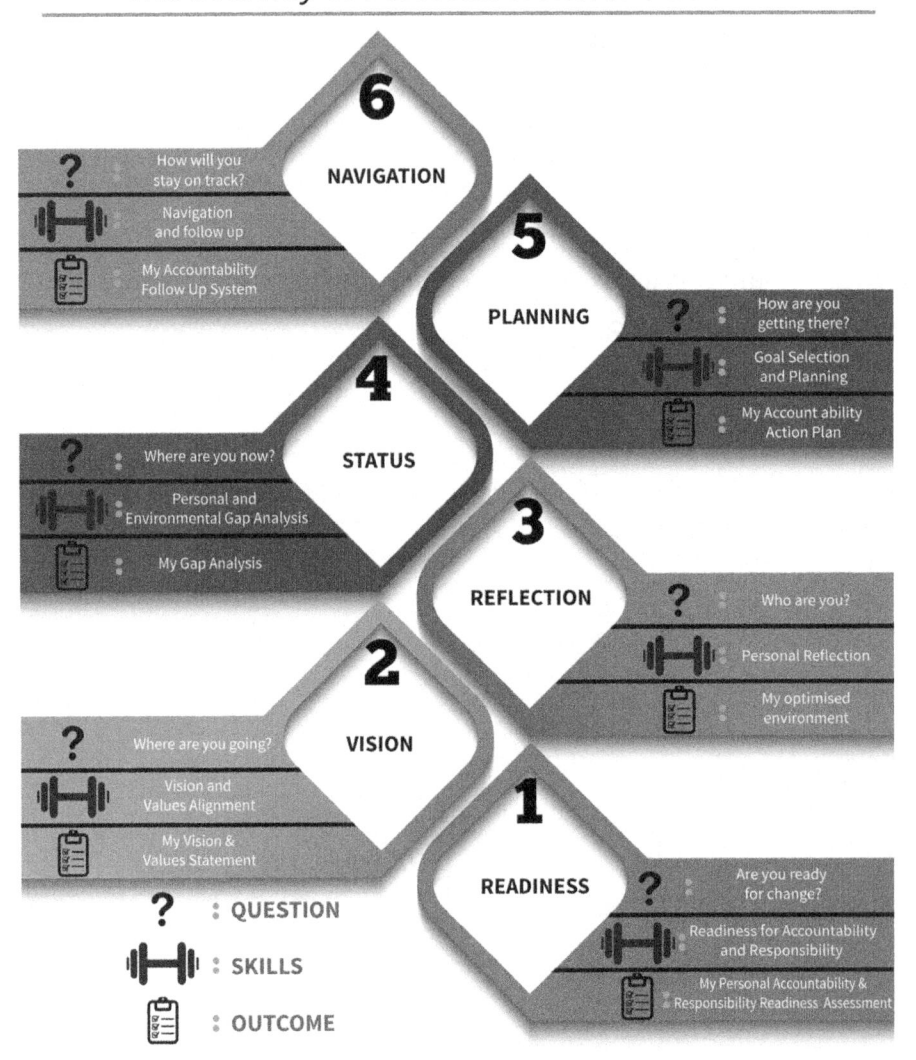

6 — NAVIGATION
- **?** How will you stay on track?
- **Skills:** Navigation and follow up
- **Outcome:** My Accountability Follow Up System

5 — PLANNING
- **?** How are you getting there?
- **Skills:** Goal Selection and Planning
- **Outcome:** My Account ability Action Plan

4 — STATUS
- **?** Where are you now?
- **Skills:** Personal and Environmental Gap Analysis
- **Outcome:** My Gap Analysis

3 — REFLECTION
- **?** Who are you?
- **Skills:** Personal Reflection
- **Outcome:** My optimised environment

2 — VISION
- **?** Where are you going?
- **Skills:** Vision and Values Alignment
- **Outcome:** My Vision & Values Statement

1 — READINESS
- **?** Are you ready for change?
- **Skills:** Readiness for Accountability and Responsibility
- **Outcome:** My Personal Accountability & Responsibility Readiness Assessment

Legend:
- **?** : QUESTION
- 🏋 : SKILLS
- 📋 : OUTCOME

Chapter Summaries

Chapter 1 The *Personal Accountability Code*™ Step 1
Answers the Question: Are You Ready for Change?

The first step to unravelling your personal accountability code is to break down your natural resistance to change by recognising just how powerful your status quo muscles can be in holding you back from your dreams and goals. Your status quo reserves are also very clever. They know you well and, rest assured, they will use that knowledge to try everything they can to fool you into giving up on what you want in life. Your status quo is particularly skilled at rubbing it in when things don't quite go to plan with comments like, '*I told you so... knew that wouldn't work... See. I told you that you would make a fool of yourself.*' The list goes on.

In this chapter, you will have the opportunity to get the better of your status quo by taking the responsibility and accountability readiness tests. The new science of accountability has revolutionised the way we see accountability and responsibility in successful goal achievement. This breakthrough has turned the context of accountability and responsibility on its head, from the traditional perspective of negative punitive measures of control into positive, principled means of growth, motivation and reward.

Raise your awareness of your strengths and development opportunities in these powerful areas, and engage an accountability partner to help you keep on track—and you will have made a fabulous start to the journey of transforming your life and career.

Exercises:
- Accountability Index (in the Guide and also available online)
- Responsibility-Readiness Assessment (in the Guide and also available online)
- Accountability Partnerships
- Celebrating the Small Stuff

Outcome:
- My Accountability and Responsibility-Readiness Assessment

Chapter 2 The *Personal Accountability Code*™ Step 2
Answers the Question: Where Are You Going?

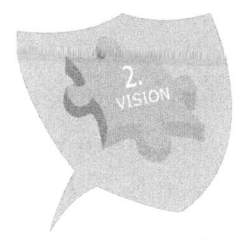

In this chapter, you get the opportunity to craft your long-term vision. Research tells us that visions inevitably fail to materialise if they are not closely aligned with your highest values. We use the new science of accountability to integrate your vision with your highest, most pressing values.

Exercises:
- Vision of the Future
- Values Exercise
- Values Prioritisation
- Vision and Values Alignment

Outcome:
- My Vision and Values Statement

Chapter 3 The *Personal Accountability Code*™ Step 3
Answers the Question: Who Are You?

In the new science of accountability, there is infinitely greater chance of being accountable for successful goal achievement if you optimise your environment to leverage your preferences and strengths. Most successful goal achievers have blind spots on their strengths, and areas for development that others see more clearly. This is why the art of asking for feedback is an important part of answering the key question of this chapter: *Who Are You?*

Exercises:
- Optimising Your Environment—What Drives You
- Optimising Your Environment—The Work Styles Assessment
- Optimising Your Environment—What Motivates You?

- Optimising Your Environment—Know Your Strengths
- The Truth About Self Discipline
- The Art of Asking for Feedback

Outcome:
- My Optimised Environment

Chapter 4 The *Personal Accountability Code*™ Step 4 Answers the Question: Where Are You Now?

In the new science of accountability, much can be learned about personal goal achievement from the fields of business planning and analysis. In this chapter, you'll take your vision to the next level and take stock of where you are right now in relation to where you want to be across several specific dimensions of your life. You'll then take a comprehensive look at the resources that are available to you, what stands in the way of your vision of the future, and what you need to have or do to get where you want to go.

Exercises:
- The Wheel of Life
- SPOT Analysis (Internal Strengths, Internal Problems, External Opportunities, External Threats)
- Strengths—Problems Gap Analysis
- Opportunities—Threats Gap Analysis
- The Truth About Habits

Outcome:
- My Gap Analysis

Chapter 5 The *Personal Accountability Code*™ Step 5
Answers the Question: How Are You Getting There?

In this chapter, you explore how the new science of accountability offers breakthrough measures in setting up a powerful action plan for successful goal choice and completion. You will take your insights from chapters 1 through 4 and create an Accountability Action Plan that is personally energising, motivating and exciting because it is tailored to your unique talents and preferences.

Exercises:
A 5-step Roadmap for Successful **SMART** Goal Achievement

- Goal Achievement Step 1—Select **Specific** Goals
- Goal Achievement Step 2—Establish **Measures** of Success
- Goal Achievement Step 3—Determine **Action** Steps
- Goal Achievement Step 4—Be **Realistic**
- Goal Achievement Step 5—Align to a **Timeframe**

Outcome:
- My Personal Accountability Action Plan

Chapter 6 The *Personal Accountability Code*™ Step 6
Answers the Question: How Will You Stay on Track?

The final piece of the successful goal achiever's *Personal Accountability Code*™ is navigating your way through your goals and priorities, and staying on track in the face of obstacles and setbacks. You will use two additional steps in the SMART + **ER** goal-achiever's model. With these final two steps 6 and 7 in play, you will have the ultimate personal accountability action plan you are unlikely to wriggle out of as soon as something goes wrong—which it will!

And what an amazing opportunity life presents us if things do go wrong. In this chapter, we also see how setbacks, obstacles and failures can be amongst our most valuable defining moments both personally and professionally—moments that can propel us into the stratosphere of personal growth and achievement.

Exercises:
The SMART+ER 7-step Process for Successful Goal Achievement:

- Goal Achievement Step 6—Ensure Goals Are **Energising**
- Goal Achievement Step 7—**Reinforce** Progress

Outcome:
- My Personal Accountability Follow-Up System

Bundle your Personal Accountability Action Plan together with your Personal Accountability Follow-Up System of staying on track, and you have unravelled your *Personal Accountability Code*™ using the *new* science of accountability—the ultimate winning strategy to designing and achieving the life and work you want for yourself.

The Accountability Coach

Solving 6 Common Dilemmas about Goal Achievement and Personal Accountability.

Appendix 1

You will find a summary of the key points of the new science of accountability in a handy checklist of the **Do's and Don'ts of** *The Personal Accountability Code*™.

Appendix 2

My Accountability Action Plan including sample goal-setting worksheets

The Personal Accountability Code

Three Editions to Choose From

In addition to the Paperback (Standard) Edition, *The Personal Accountability Code*™ is also available in Paperback (Premium) and Kindle editions.

The Paperback (Premium) Edition offers the convenience of a workbook PLUS the flexibility of secure access to a bonus on-line tool for customising and printing your own *Personal Accountability Code*™ Report and *Accountability Action Plan*.

The Kindle E-book Edition is a convenient quick start option, accessible via a kindle reader, or a tablet, smart phone or computer uploaded with Amazon's free kindle reading software application.

How to Use This Guide

1. Have a personal journal or notebook and a pen available.
2. Open your copy of *The Personal Accountability Code*™ (Paperback) Edition.
3. Work step-by-step through the exercises in the *Code* and record your answers either in the blank spaces supplied in the workbook or in your journal/notebook.

Upgrading to The Personal Accountability Code™ (Premium) Edition

Purchasers of *The Personal Accountability Code*™ (Standard) Paperback Edition may unlock the additional on-line reporting functionality of the Premium Edition by purchasing an Upgrade (Kindle) Edition. *The Personal Accountability Code*™ *Upgrade: User Guide* can be found at the Amazon kindle store.

THE PERSONAL ACCOUNTABILITY CODE™

Step 1: Are You Ready for Change?

1. READINESS

Purpose of This Chapter

In this chapter, you will have the opportunity to take the responsibility and accountability readiness tests. The new science of accountability has revolutionised the way we see accountability and responsibility in the dynamics of successful goal achievement. This breakthrough has turned the context of accountability and responsibility on its head from the traditional perspective of negative punitive measures of control into positive, principled means of growth, motivation and reward.

Raise your awareness of your strengths and development opportunities in these powerful areas and engage an accountability partner to help you keep on track, and you will have made a fabulous start to the journey of redesigning your life.

By the end of this Chapter, you will have completed the following exercises:

- Responsibility-Readiness Assessment (in workbook and also available online)
- Accountability Index (in workbook and also available online)
- Accountability Partnerships
- Celebrating the Small Stuff

Are You Ready for Change?

How many psychologists does it take to change a light bulb? In the old joke, it takes only one psychologist to change a light bulb, but it has to *want to change* first. It's commonly held knowledge that to change any behaviour, one has to first be aware of it and experience the pain that it brings.

It's like that with accountability and responsibility. You go along using familiar excuses until one day you realise that even your really, truly good excuses aren't satisfying you anymore. *You're the one* not achieving what you say you really want.

Once you decide that excuses aren't working for you like you'd hoped, you can start to take responsibility for doing something about it, achieving your goals and creating the life you really *do* want.

Or, you can make up some better excuses. You choose.

Write down your definitions of 'accountability' and 'responsibility':

_____

_____

Responsibility vs. Accountability

Although the terms 'responsibility' and 'accountability' are often used interchangeably, they actually have very different meanings. For clarity, think of responsibility as your willingness to own your role and participation in a situation.

Accountability describes in specific terms exactly who will do what by when. It is, as the root word 'account' implies, something you can track and keep account of.

Another way of differentiating between the two is to think in terms of how we deliver on our promises:

> *'...Accountability...refers to the capacity of one person to hold another to account for the delivery of their promises. Responsibility, on the other hand, is one's individual capacity to deliver on the promises they make.'*
> **Accountability Leadership (2013) Di Worrall**

When you are *responsible*, you don't look to assign fault, blame, or find excuses. Instead, you focus on finding solutions. Being responsible means starting to look at tasks and challenges as an opportunity to produce good results.

- If I fail, then what do I need to learn and do differently?
- If you fail, how can we help each other learn, correct and move on?

I can't be accountable to anyone unless I take responsibility for my outcomes. Neither can you. If everyone's mired in excuses, blame and finding fault, then we don't have time and energy for getting the right things done right.

A Union of Responsibility *and* Accountability: *'Response—Account—Ability'*

Responsibility cannot function well without accountability—and vice versa. We require a balance of both competencies: *'Response—Account—Ability'* to achieve a healthy, successful and productive life.

Do You Really *Want* to Change?

Describe a time when you had to make a change. Was it easy or difficult for you?

_____

_____

The reality is and always has been that *it is your choice to change.* It's your life, your career, your attitude, your family. The people I know who are truly successful and happy have all but discarded their excuses in favour of taking responsibility and being personally accountable for their outcomes where it matters most.

The only person you can be responsible for and really change is *you*. Most of us are pretty crafty about getting around that with minimal of work and effort, but it all comes back to personal accountability.

Without taking responsibility, you can't change anything—you can't change yourself, and you certainly can't influence others to change or be accountable if you're not.

But how do you improve your accountability and responsibility skills?

Almost everyone I talk with perceives themselves to be highly responsible and accountable in most situations. Very few admit to being irresponsible and unaccountable.

After all, a certain level of responsibility and accountability is required to function in life and at work. But in reality there can be a gap between how we *perceive* our capabilities in this regard and our *actual* behaviour.

So before you start creating any sort of plan for achieving your goals, start with the following exercises, to determine your personal readiness for responsibility.

How Ready Are You for Responsibility?

Reflect on a situation when you held yourself accountable for delivering on your responsibilities.

- ❒ Did you find this easy or difficult? Why?

_____
_____
_____
_____
_____
_____
_____
_____
_____
_____

- ❒ Describe an incident where you sidestepped your responsibility and instead deferred to using blame and excuses for something that didn't go to plan (maybe you called them 'rational explanations'?). Why did you find this difficult? It is hard for most peo-

The Personal Accountability Code

ple to recognise their own lack of accountability. If needed, ask a trusted co-worker or close friend to help to identify an example.

_____
_____
_____
_____
_____
_____
_____
_____
_____
_____

- ☐ Can you find any patterns? Do you have a tendency to avoid responsibility when you lack motivation? When do you most often find yourself using excuses or blaming others?

_____
_____
_____
_____
_____
_____
_____
_____
_____
_____

Now fill in the Responsibility-Readiness Assessment, which will help you determine how ready you are to take full responsibility for making positive changes in your life.

Hint: *You can take the assessment here or online at* **http://www.theaccountabilitycode.com.au**

The Responsibility-Readiness Assessment

		1	2	3	4	5
\multicolumn{7}{l}{*Rate your level of agreement with the following statements on a scale from 1 to 5, where: 1 = Disagree; 2 = Somewhat Disagree; 3 = Don't Know; 4 = Somewhat Agree; 5 = Agree*}
1.	I am responsible for my success and happiness.					
2.	I clarify what others expect from me on an ongoing basis.					
3.	I clarify what I expect from others regularly. Even when I delegate a task, I remain ultimately responsible for ensuring its completion.					
4.	Before I agree to and begin a task, I plan for difficulties and obstacles that might happen.					
5.	I clearly understand my skills and ask for help when needed.					
6.	I hold myself accountable and avoid using excuses and blame to deflect my contribution if something goes wrong.					
7.	When things don't go to plan, I am more likely to seek out new solutions than give up.					
8.	When there are interpersonal problems, I believe in having conversations even though they may be difficult. I try to assume good intentions from others.					
9.	It is important to give myself positive recognition for the progress I make towards my goals.					
10.	I ask for feedback regularly and keep an open mind.					
\multicolumn{2}{l}{*Add up the scores in each column, then record the total score below:*}					
\multicolumn{7}{l}{**Total Score:**}

The Personal Accountability Code

Score of 40 or more: If your responses add up to 40 or more, you are living a high level of personal responsibility. You accept that your choices and behaviours are creating your outcomes. You have a responsibility mindset and are prepared to take action on a Personal Accountability Plan.

You most likely have a personal definition of success, both for your work and personal life. You are also likely to be comfortable seeking to clarify what others expect from you. You can make your expectations of yourself and the expectations that others have of you even more clear by writing them down, if you haven't already. *Clear agreements, even when created for yourself, create trust and credibility for holding yourself and others accountable.*

You understand that continual learning and refining of interpersonal skills will help you succeed. You are ready to commit to owning your role in designing and accomplishing your goals and plans.

Action Steps for you

Congratulations. You are ready for responsibility. Not only do you have a strong responsibility and accountability mindset, you are also in a position to model responsibility and coach others in its application. You are ready to assess how you rate on holding others accountable for outcomes.

My reflection on the Responsibility-Readiness Assessment:

_____
_____
_____
_____
_____
_____

Score of 30-40: If your responses add up to 30–40, you are already accepting 60–70% responsibility for the choices you make, your behaviours and results. You have great potential to expand your capabilities even further and develop the accountability mindset that will help you fulfil your responsibilities, change your life and guarantee even further success.

You have developed some strong skills in personal accountability and responsibility, yet there are times when you choose not to take full ownership of a situation.

My Action Steps

Reflect on a circumstance for which you were/are satisfied that you took/are taking full responsibility. How does that make you feel?

What are the benefits or payoffs you or others experience from you taking this position?

_____
_____

Give yourself some acknowledgement for accepting responsibility.

_____
_____

Is there is a current situation in which you feel contracted by not taking on full responsibility? If so,

    a. What is the situation?
    b. What is it costing you in personal health, happiness or goal achievement?
    c. What is the benefit or payoff of not taking full responsibility?
    d. Is it something you want to change? (On a score of 1-10, write your willingness to change your response in this situation, where 1 is not at all and 10 is definitely yes)
    e. If yes when?
    f. What can you do now to take one step forward in tackling this issue?

Tips for improving your readiness for responsibility

1. Be willing to look at what's working in your life and what's not. You might want to work with a professional coach or a designated accountability partner to define what success looks like. How can you improve your success and make more progress?
2. Put important responsibilities in writing. This will clarify expectations and help you eliminate the potential for excuses and blame.
3. Involve trusted others with your progress. Ask them to help you identify what triggers those moments of poor responsibility and how they can support you to improve your responsibility skills at such times.

Score of up to 30: If your scores are 30 or below, you accept some responsibility for your successes and failures; however, you tend to go with what life dishes out, viewing yourself as a victim of circumstances. You see many of your problems as someone else's fault. While some of this may in fact be true, it doesn't help you to change things. You end up being stuck in a vicious circle—a passive recipient of what life has to offer rather than being in the driver's seat influencing outcomes.

My Action Steps

Is there is a current situation in which you feel contracted by not taking on full responsibility? If so,

   a. What is the situation?
   b. What is it costing you in personal health, happiness or goal achievement?
   c. What is the benefit or payoff of not taking full responsibility?
   d. Is it something you want to change? (On a score of 1-10, write your willingness to change your response in this situation, where 1 is not at all and 10 is definitely yes)
   e. If yes when?
   f. What can you do now to take one step forward in tackling this issue?

_____

Tips for improving your readiness for responsibility

I suspect you have some level of dissatisfaction with how things are going for you, since you've come this far in taking the responsibility-readiness assessment. If this is the case for you, the first step in turning this situation around is to look at your role in creating the results you are currently experiencing.

   1. Enlist the help you need—a friend, family or, even better, a professional coach. It can be difficult to see your own role in creating your outcomes. Find someone who

can give you an honest appraisal of the current situation, help you see what's possible, help you to define for yourself what you want, and help you to get moving.

2. Don't fool yourself about going it alone. Invite support. Personal responsibility *CAN be coached.* Find an accountability partner with whom you can share the journey.

Now move on to the next section, on The Secrets of Highly Successful (and Accountable) People.

The Secrets of Highly Successful (and Accountable) People

No one lives and works in total isolation. While personal success means that you often need to hold yourself to account for delivering on your responsibilities, rarely do you function alone. Everyone functions in the context of relationships. We need other people to help us achieve our goals—be that a family, a social group or business organisation. The skill of holding others accountable for delivering on their promises is just as important as holding *ourselves* accountable for results. And that skill doesn't just apply to leaders. The capacity to enlist support and delegate where necessary applies to any member of a team or group in which the individuals depend on each other to get things done.

In this section, you will have the opportunity to fill in the Personal Accountability Index to help you self-assess your habitual ways of interacting with other people and what this means for your skills in accountability.

In my executive coaching experience, even the most seasoned CEO can improve his or her ability to hold others accountable for outcomes. In reality, most people are reticent about reminding others of obligations, especially colleagues when 'It's not my job!' or it risks conflict.

Even when it *is* your job, it's difficult for many people to provide meaningful corrective feedback. Practically everyone—managers, supervisors, friends, and parents—can improve their ability to hold themselves and others accountable.

It doesn't mean we would like to see everyone turn into 'The Accountability Police'. That wouldn't be much fun, nor would it bring about the kind of success that comes from working together harmoniously.

Holding High-Accountability Conversations

How do you rate your level of comfort and skill in holding others accountable? Do you find yourself sometimes reticent to speak up because you don't want to come across as negative? Perhaps you don't want to risk ruining a relationship or hurting someone's feelings. This is very common. Most of us want to be accepted and loved, not perceived as critical and harsh.

Think about a conversation you have (or avoid) with others. Is there a burning issue that you are uncomfortable to address and that stops you from speaking up and holding others accountable?

_____

_____

I believe that many people have never learned the 'language of accountability'. Without the confidence that comes with mastering such a skill, many individuals I know 'wait and see'. They put off the conversation in the hope that things will work themselves out.

To make matters worse, should that situation escalate to the point where it can no longer be ignored or put off and we are forced to hold someone to account over an uncomfortable matter, then it's almost too late to have a conversation that will get things back on track. Our lack of practice means that the conversation is often clunky and uncomfortable. Emotions fly, words aren't chosen carefully, and it's almost certain that relationships and trust become damaged.

The solution is to help each other out by holding focused accountability conversations when it matters most.

Accountability is a two-way street. It almost never goes in just one direction, even between manager and employee. Think about it: the boss asks the employee to complete tasks. And the employee asks for tools, training and a pay cheque. Each holds the other to account for delivering on their responsibilities.

Don't underestimate the power of a good conversation. You can build trust, cooperation, respect, and light up enthusiasm and energy. It may not always be easy to hold accountability conversations, but done well, everyone gains and life is easier.

The Personal Accountability Code

If you want to vastly improve your ability to succeed in life, pay attention to how you ask others to be accountable. Take the following survey to assess how comfortable you are in holding high-accountability conversations.

Hint: You can fill in the Personal Accountability Index here or online at **www.theaccountabilitycode.com**

Personal Accountability Index

Agree	Don't Agree	
		Once I give a task to someone else, it becomes their responsibility if something goes wrong.
		When asking others for input, I believe it's a good idea to have a well-thought-out solution in mind at the outset.
		Even though I give clear instructions and requests, I'm often disappointed that people don't deliver to my expectations.
		I find it preferable to work around other people's failings rather than call them on it because I value good relationships over unnecessary confrontation and upset.
		If I purchase an item or service that has minor defects, I'm unlikely to send it back, because it's not worth the drama.
		I often find myself resorting to the fact that if I want something done properly, I may as well do it myself.
		When someone consistently fails to deliver, I'm unlikely to call them on it immediately as things usually work themselves out.
		If I see someone who's clearly in the wrong, I have a hard time telling them in a way that won't make them angry and defensive.
		When someone misses a committed deadline, I will let them off the hook even when they didn't let me know in time.
		When someone appears unable to do a task, or complains about it, I usually jump in with my advice about how to do it properly.

Scoring: Add up the total number of 'Disagree' Scores. Maximum personal accountability = 10.

If you scored 8 to 10, you have developed a strong accountability mindset together with solid skills in holding others accountable for delivering on their promises. You are comfortable with the language of accountability and are likely to be a role model for others. You can confidently ask for assistance and delegate key tasks to others in order to achieve your goals.

Compare your personal responsibility scores with your accountability scores. Talk with your coach or accountability partner about the possibility that you may feel overly responsible and reticent to delegate or ask for help. Remember that you can learn to share tasks, involve others and achieve much more when you do.

Continue to work with others to achieve your goals and help them achieve theirs. Even the most accomplished of leaders have coaches or accountability partners who help them pursue their personal development goals. Consider working with an accountability partner to help you address your blind spots or issues you might be consciously or unconsciously avoiding.

My accountability development objectives…

_____
_____
_____
_____
_____
_____
_____
_____
_____

The Personal Accountability Code

If you scored 6 to 8, you can identify specific situations in which you have demonstrated solid skills in confidently holding others accountable and delegating tasks. There are other circumstances in which you might find yourself avoiding a conversation or failing to follow someone up on a task, hoping things will resolve themselves. Sometimes you might hear yourself blaming someone or making excuses for an outcome that didn't turn out as planned even though you shared overall responsibility with that person/s.

Compare your personal responsibility scores with your accountability scores. Talk with your coach or accountability partner about the possibility that you may be using delegation as a means of avoiding personal responsibility in some situations. Remember that, just because you delegate a task, it does not mean that you have deflected responsibility for its outcome.

Work with a trusted accountability partner or coach to uncover the 'triggers' that cause you to avoid accountability conversations and behaviours. These triggers will be obstacles that prevent you from achieving your goals, so it is important that you draw up a personal development plan that will help you close your accountability 'gaps' where it matters the most.

Draw upon your existing skills in the mindset and language of accountability to boost your confidence.

My accountability development objectives…

_____
_____
_____
_____
_____
_____
_____
_____
_____
_____

If you scored 1 to 5, you probably find yourself feeling victimised and not in control of the outcomes you desire. Even though you may have burning issues you would like to address with other people (either to do something or stop doing something), there are times when the thought of raising the issue is too uncomfortable.

You often find yourself reticent to speak up because you don't want to come across as negative and cause a confrontation. Perhaps you don't want to risk ruining a relationship or hurting someone's feelings. Know that these feelings are very common. Most of us want to be accepted and loved, not perceived as critical and harsh.

It is true that developing the skills of accountability can feel daunting. It also true that to continue to live with the stress of victimisation and feeling that you are not in control of your life goals is unhealthy for your physical and mental health. That's why we recommend you identify the issues involving other people that you would like to work on the most. Engage with a trusted coach or accountability partner to help create an action plan to help you develop your accountability muscles in this area.

(Please note that whenever you find personal stress escalating at work, it's a signal that something is not functioning well. Remember that sometimes we need to ask for special assistance where our personal health or safety is at risk.)

My accountability development objectives…

_____
_____
_____
_____
_____
_____
_____
_____
_____
_____

How to Work on Your 'Accountability Ability'

These assessment tools are meant to raise your awareness of the common traps we fall into when it comes to responsibility and accountability. There are no quick fixes and easy solutions, but there are simple steps you can take to make a significant difference in achieving your life and career plans.

It's important that you identify your areas for improvement. An accountability partner or coach can be a great resource for this exercise. In the next section, we look at how coaching and accountability partnerships work, and give you a system for using these relationships to help grow your skills in personal responsibility and accountability.

Accountability Partnerships

Commitments and goals are easier to keep when you share them with a trusted partner. You are more likely to stay the course and work harder when you have someone to be accountable to.

Two of the most successful personal behavioural change programs in the world are Weight Watchers and Alcoholics Anonymous. The reason individuals find success in losing weight and quitting alcohol has a lot to do with personal accountability being integrated into the social elements of both these programs. People show up at meetings, assess where they are, accept where they are and get support from others to make regular progress.

From the perspective of professional career development, the Marshall Goldsmith Stakeholder-Centered Coaching process is a global program recognised for measurable behavioural change in business leaders. The success of this program is largely due to the systemic alignment of the leader's goals with stakeholder expectations. It is the leader's key stakeholders who essentially become the leader's community of accountability coaches.

Accountability works for long-term ingrained habits and addictions, and it can work for you, to improve whatever you're dissatisfied with in your life and work. But those who succeed most are those who get support and help through others.

An accountability partner is a person who helps you keep a commitment. You can choose a friend, mentor, trusted colleague, business stakeholder or professional coach. You set up an agreement and the person coaches, supports, and helps remind you of the agreement.

It should be someone who isn't afraid to call you on your self-talk, excuses, and explanations. They should be able to speak with you honestly without disturbing the relationship trust. But it also takes a degree of courage and determination on your part to ask for help and consider their suggestions with grace and appreciation.

Accountability partnerships truly do work, as long as you have a trusting relationship. But it does require regular contact, either by phone, email or face-to-face. They can be set up in a variety of ways, such as brief daily check-ins on personal targets or monthly check-ins for more complex professional goals.

Accountability partnerships are similar to peer-coaching relationships. There can be mutual accountability. One of the most successful coaches in the world, Marshall Goldsmith, checks in daily with a trusted colleague. Here's how:

Marshall Goldsmith's Daily Questions

Accountability is a key ingredient in a successful Peer Coaching relationship. How often you check in with each other depends on your schedules and how you've set up your goals. The most effective method we've found for staying on track and making maximum progress is what we call 'Daily Questions'.

Andrew Thorn introduced Marshall to this idea. After trying it out with Andrew, Marshall continued the practice with his good friend Jim Moore, former CLO of Sun Microsystems, Nortel and BellSouth. Both Marshall and Jim report amazing results.

THE **PERSONAL** ACCOUNTABILITY CODE

> Every day, Jim asks Marshall the same 24 questions. Every day, Marshall asks Jim the same 17 questions. Marshall and Jim each have a spreadsheet of each other's questions where they record for each other the answers: 'yes', 'no', or a number. Structuring the questions in this way keeps the phone call moving. Each phone call lasts only a couple of minutes. They send each other their completed spreadsheets weekly. If they miss a day or two, they simply 'catch up' later.
>
> Some keys:
>
> - Each person writes their own questions.
> - No negative feedback. No comments that might produce any form of guilt.
> - Yes to positive feedback! If you can make positive comments to reinforce success, by all means, go ahead!
>
> Ask Questions Daily from **www. Marshall Goldsmith Library.com**

Sample Daily Questions

These aren't the same as your goals, but of course they should align with them. Think of them as daily steps in your personal development plan that will bring you closer to your goals. In one example, an executive wanted to play jazz piano, but found daily practice hard. After she set up daily accountability phone calls with a fellow student, the task became easier and more fun.

Listing daily questions is a good way to jump right into a program to improve accountability. It'll build your accountability muscles! Try it out and see what happens.

Here's a few of Marshall Goldsmith's daily questions:

- 'Have I done my 100 sit-ups?'
- 'Did I say or do anything nice for my wife?'
- 'How many minutes did I write?'

Here are some other examples:

- Did I eat three healthy meals of moderate portions today?
- Did I ask at least one socially oriented question of my staff?
- Did I complete my reports?
- Was I on time for my meetings?
- Did I listen more than I talked today?

These are questions that can be answered yes or no or a number. In some cases, you can add a percentage to estimate how much was actually completed. It's up to you.

The reason accountability partnerships work is we are inherently social beings. We want to be perceived as congruent between what we say and what we do. It's easier to make excuses to ourselves in private than to admit to a friend we haven't followed through.

If you decide to run with an accountability partner (and I highly recommend that you do), decide who you'd like to approach, and ask them to participate. They may have something they want you to help them with, thereby setting up a mutually beneficial arrangement.

Using Daily Questions to Work With Your Accountability Partner or Coach

In the responsibility-readiness assessment and accountability index, you identified some key action steps to improve your skills in both responsibility and accountability. Working with your accountability partner or coach to help you follow up on these action items can be a good start to your accountability partnership. Referring to your action items, identify at least three things you could put on your list of daily accountability questions:

1. _____
2. _____
3. _____

Tips for Choosing Your Accountability Partner

This is REALLY important. Shared values are the foundation of a good-quality accountability partnership. Consider selecting candidates you know, but who are from outside your inner circle. Close friends and family will not be neutral. You want someone who will hold your feet to the fire but without judging or arguing with you.

Think of people you already know with whom you have a good relationship. Ask yourself:

- Does this person share similar values to me?
- Do they meet what I am looking for in an accountability partner?
- Do I have a good, positive connection with that person?
- Do I think that person might be interested in the idea?

Considering the above points, write down three to five people you'd consider asking to be an accountability partner:

1. _____
2. _____
3. _____
4. _____
5. _____

Now go back and rank each one in order, from 1st preference to 5th preference.

How to Ask Someone If They Would Be Willing to Be Your Accountability Partner

When you have answered these questions fully, approach the person you are considering. Don't just hit them with 'Do you want to be my accountability partner?' Present the idea and ask if it is something they are interested in exploring further. Have a discussion about the potential benefits and results for both of you. Brainstorm ideas that would be appropriate and that work for you.

The key here is to make it a discussion—not a 'will you/won't you?' ultimatum. Engage in conversation.

If they say yes, great. Game on. Work out a format that works for both of you—and off you go.

If they say it isn't for them, just thank them for considering it and move on. Go back to your contact list and follow the same process again.

Tips for Setting up an Accountability Partnership

Now that you have a shortlist of who you would like to ask to be your accountability partner, and how to ask them, here are some tips for setting up a successful accountability partnership:

- **Set clear boundaries** and expectations. Decide who will call whom, at what time, on which days. Outline your process: 'Hello, this is me. I'm letting you know I completed five out of my six assignments and I plan to finish the other one tomorrow morning.' An accountability partner is not a receptacle for your excuses.
- **Keep your word.** The buddy system only works when you use it well. It's not coaching, nor is it a place to vent your excuses. When necessary, admit you've not done what you said you would, make another plan, and recommit.
- **Use a document.** A spreadsheet will allow you to track what's done and what's partially done. Don't rely on your memory. It will shift in your favour over time. Your memory isn't a good accountability partner.

Tips for Working with a Coach

If you find the notion of approaching an accountability partner too difficult, ask yourself if you're ready to commit to making the changes you say you'd like. Perhaps you're not as ready as you'd like to be. If you feel this is the case, consider working with a coach who can help improve your readiness for the responsibility of making changes in your life.

While peer accountability partners are invaluable for helping you stay on track, they are not professional coaches. Professional career and life coaches, on the other hand, can function as accountability partners and also offer the benefits of being qualified to improve your skills through the journey of goal achievement.

Why Engage a Career or Life Coach?

Books and information are one form of learning. Training classes even better. But coaching which takes place on the canvas of real-life experiences as they unfold is the highest form of learning and development with the greatest likelihood of supporting real change in behaviour and results.

Specifically, a career or life coach can:

- Partner with you to convert the learning from *The Personal Accountability Code*™ into the reality of everyday life
- Establish a safe, trusting, empathetic and non-judgemental environment in which you can confidentially explore your hopes and dreams
- Ask you questions, provide insights, and offer professional techniques and assessment tools that enable you to see yourself more clearly—your strengths and weaknesses and areas for capability development
- Challenge you to raise the bar
- Support you to create agreements around your goals, and plans for their achievement
- Help you to anticipate, prepare for and deal with obstacles that arise
- Create a structure and framework of accountability to help you stay on track

You can also find coaches with more specific specialties, such as executive leadership coaching, to bring about improvements in leadership behaviour and organisational performance.

What a coach doesn't do

It's easy to blame someone or something else when things go wrong.

Unfortunately, it is also true that those closest to us can be our primary targets when we are on the lookout for someone else to blame. Friends, family and colleagues can suffer the brunt of our frustration. Strangely, those who are in a role to support and guide us such as coaches can be particularly vulnerable to the receiving end of our rants when times get tough.

But being accountable is about taking responsibility for our own action or inaction, successes and failures. It is never up to someone else—including professional coaches to make us "transform". That privilege is ours and ours alone to experience.

To quote Marshall Goldsmith, the highest rated executive coach on the Thinkers50 List in both 2011 and 2013:

> *"Too many people think that a coach—especially an accomplished one—will solve their problems. That's like thinking that you'll get in shape by hiring the world's best trainer and not working out yourself."*
> **It's Not About the Coach (2004), www.marshallgoldsmithlibrary.com/articles**

If you've not worked with a coach before, start asking around for a referral from friends and associates. Or go online. There are organisations that certify coaches in your area.

☐ Research and write down the names of some coaches you could contact:
   1. _____
   2. _____
   3. _____

☐ Write out what you want to say and how you will say it. An example would be, 'Hi, my name is… and I was referred by… I'm looking to work with a coach. I am planning on identifying and working on some goals. Can you tell me about your services?' Then… do it—make that call and have those conversations. Just do it.

_____
_____
_____
_____
_____
_____
_____

THE **PERSONAL** ACCOUNTABILITY CODE

It's the Small Wins That Count

In the new science of accountability, ***one of the secrets to sustaining motivation is to recognise small wins along the way.***

If you made it all the way through the tasks assigned in this preparation chapter, take a moment to congratulate yourself for unravelling the first part of your personal accountability code.

The first step is often the most difficult.

Write down what steps you've already taken, and take a few moments to realise you're not starting from scratch. You've already prepared the way.

Here's what you've done so far—congratulations!

_____
_____
_____
_____
_____
_____
_____
_____
_____
_____
_____
_____
_____
_____
_____

Checklist for Chapter 1—Am I Ready For Change?

☐ I have taken the **Responsibility-Readiness Assessment.**

☐ I have **written down some action steps that will help me improve my readiness for responsibility.**

☐ I have completed my **Personal Accountability Index**.

☐ I have written down some objectives for **improving my accountability 'ability'**

☐ I am finding an **accountability partner or coach** to work with.

☐ I have taken a moment to **recognise my progress** so far.

☐ I have made a list of **daily questions** I can ask myself or have my accountability partner/coach ask me.

THE PERSONAL ACCOUNTABILITY CODE™

Step 2: Where Are You Going?

2. VISION

THE **PERSONAL** ACCOUNTABILITY CODE

Purpose of This Chapter

Before you launch into choosing a goal to work on, make sure it's something that matters to you. It should get you to where you truly want to go. To find out what you really want, it is important that you take a step back to look at the big picture and ask yourself: *'What is my vision of an ideal life?'*

In Step 2 of *The Personal Accountability Code*™, you have the opportunity to explore your personal vision and record the future you want for yourself, in work and in life.

After completing the worksheets in this chapter, I'd like to see you:

- Inspired to take action on a clear vision of your future
- Energised by the most important personal values that naturally ignite your passion and align with your personal vision
- Clear about your core values and how to align these to your goals and tasks for maximum satisfaction and momentum

Crystallise Your Purpose by Crafting Your Vision of the Future

'If you don't stand for something, you'll fall for anything.'

Why have your own vision of the future? Because a vision captures the essence of purpose and meaning in your life.

What is your vision of the future?

Few people take the time to write down their plans—but those who do are more likely to succeed.

Step 2: Where Are You Going?

To create the future you want and achieve your goals, it's essential to write it down. A study by Dominican University reveals those who had written down their goals dramatically increased their success rate from 43% to 61% over those who didn't write them down.[1]

In life and work, we tend to get mired in day-to-day tasks. Those who maintain their energy and motivation are usually those who connect tasks to a bigger picture. Are you doing this? Do you have a profoundly inspiring purpose anchored by a vision that can help you stay accountable to your dreams when things get routine or stressful?

A powerful vision can inspire great things—for people in pursuit of personal goals, as well as for managers and leaders guiding groups of people with shared goals. In fact, visioning is one of the top traits that successful leaders develop. It's what distinguishes great leaders from the mediocre.

If you are in a position of leadership, people look to you to show them the future of the department, organisation, or project. They expect you to understand and discuss the big picture with them, helping them connect with a common vision of the future. People need and appreciate a sense of direction, especially in times of change.

Whether you use *The Personal Accountability Code*™ for your personal development goals, or to pursue family oriented, community or career goals, the process of crafting a vision is the vital first step across all these applications, which must occur before the first goal is determined.

This holds true for individuals as well as groups or teams of people in families, community or business. A shared vision has the power to inspire people to accept responsibility and hold each other accountable. Vision statements provide the glue that gives people energy and a reason to care.

In the next section, you will use the Visioning Tool to craft a vision of your ideal future.

---

1   Writing Down Goals Study:
    1) **http://cdn.sidsavara.com/wp-content/uploads/2008/09/researchsummary2.pdf**
    2) **http://www.fastcompany.com/1798754/goals-difference-between-success-and-failure**

The Visioning Tool

Instructions: Consider the big picture with the following three questions.

Over the course of your life:

1. Who would you like to be? E.g. happy, fulfilled, responsible
2. What would you like to do? E.g. travel, volunteer, study
3. What would you like to have? E.g. a home, a healthy bank account

Now, get a little more specific and describe a vision of your ideal future by telling a story. Complete this exercise alone and then with your coach/accountability partner. Tell your story in as much detail as possible.

Tell Your Story

Fast forward three to five years and imagine you are being interviewed by a journalist about the achievements you are proud of and the path you took to get there. You can choose any or all aspects of your life, whether they be personal, career, health & fitness, family, spiritual or your community pursuits. Use the following series of questions to tell your story in as much detail as possible. Be as creative as you like. There are no right or wrong answers.

❐ What is it like in the future—Where are you? What are you doing? Who is in your life? What does it feel like? What does it look like?

_____
_____
_____
_____
_____
_____
_____
_____

Step 2: Where Are You Going?

- ☐ What successes did you achieve that you are most proud of? How did you measure your success? What evidence did you have?

- ☐ What did you learn that you would do the same or differently?

- ☐ What was the vision that led you to this future?

The Personal Accountability Code

Now step back from the future and return to the present, answering the following question: On a scale of 1–10, how motivated are you today to go for this vision, where 10 is highly motivated and 1 is unmotivated? (Circle the number that best applies)

1 2 3 4 5 6 7 8 9 10

Why not higher?

What resources or support would it take to motivate you to increase that score by half to 1 point?

_____
_____
_____
_____
_____
_____
_____
_____

The Values Exercise

Have you ever set out to achieve something, only to struggle and give up because your enthusiasm died out? When goals turn into hard work, we re-evaluate how much we really care. When that happens, it's likely that your intentions were not aligned with your core values.

Values can be defined as a broad preference for appropriate courses of action or outcomes. As such, values reflect a person's sense of right and wrong and what 'ought' to be.

Personal values provide an internal reference for what is good, beneficial, important, useful, beautiful, desirable, constructive, and/or ethical. Values generate behaviours that help solve common problems and provide answers for why people do what they do and in what order they choose to do them.

It's really important to identify your core personal values because whenever you do something that is closely aligned with what you value most, you'll find amazing energy and passion. If you attempt to achieve tasks that are misaligned with your values, it can be difficult to sustain motivation and drive. This is the root cause of many failures in personal goal achievement.

When you know what literally turns you on and ignites your fire, you'll be able to use this as motivation to create *flow* conditions. You'll find 'the zone'; you'll work without hesitation and it will seem more like play. You'll be able to tap into your inner drive and values to achieve tasks, projects and goals that matter most to you.

My Habitual Behaviours

Uncover the values that are important to you by answering the following simple questions about your most habitual behaviours[2]:

☐ How do you fill the space where you live?

_____
_____
_____
_____
_____
_____

☐ What do you spend your time doing?

_____
_____
_____
_____
_____
_____

---

2 Uncovering Habitual Behaviours: *A Climate for Change* (2009) by Di Worrall, Life Success Publishing. Adapted from *The Breakthrough Experience* (2002) by J. Demartini, Hay House.

The **Personal** Accountability Code

- ☐ What do you spend your money on?

- ☐ What do you naturally think about and like talking about?

- ☐ Where are you easily the most disciplined?

STEP 2: WHERE ARE YOU GOING?

_____
_____
_____
_____
_____
_____
_____
_____

My Values

Your most habitual behaviours reveal much about your innermost values. Look at the following list of values and select the top three to five that you feel are most likely driving the behaviours you just described:

- ☐ **Power**: authority; leadership; dominance
- ☐ **Achievement**: success; capability; ambition; influence; intelligence; self-respect
- ☐ **Hedonism**: pleasure; enjoying life
- ☐ **Stimulation**: daring activities; varied life; exciting life
- ☐ **Self-direction**: creativity; freedom; independence; curiosity; choosing your own goals
- ☐ **Universalism**: broadmindedness; wisdom; social justice; equality; a world at peace; a world of beauty; unity with nature; protecting the environment; inner harmony
- ☐ **Benevolence**: helpfulness; honesty; forgiveness; loyalty; responsibility; friendship
- ☐ **Tradition:** accepting one's position in life; humility; devoutness; respect for tradition; moderation
- ☐ **Conformity**: self-discipline; obedience
- ☐ **Security**: cleanliness; family security; national security; stability of social order; reciprocation of favours; health; sense of belonging
- ☐ **Spirituality**: 'The goal of finding meaning in life'

S. H. Schwartz, 1994

Once you identify what truly matters to you, look at how you are expressing these strengths and virtues in your daily life. In the following section, prioritise the values you listed by selecting your top three values in order of most important to least important in terms of how you wish to live your life.

Prioritising My Values

Priority 1—Why this value is the most important to me:

Priority 2—Why this value truly matters to me:

Priority 3—Why this value truly matters to me:

Reflect on the values you have chosen. Are they aligned with and supportive of the vision statement you created? For example, if you state that your vision in five years is to be working in business marketing, you can include values by stating your reasons why: *'In five years, I'll be using my creativity in business marketing for a top high-tech company using leading-edge tools and principles.'*

This vision statement reveals several core values:

- Achievement
- Stimulation
- Self-direction

Your personal vision carries the most impact if it is congruent with your highest values. Review your vision statement and revise it to include your most important values:

My Personal Vision and Values Statement

Checklist for Chapter 2—Where Am I Going?

☐ I have **crafted a compelling vision** for my future in at least one area of my life—personal, family, health & fitness, career, etc.

☐ I have **identified the top 3-5 values** that drive my behaviours and have prioritised them in order of importance.

☐ I've **written a vision statement** that is aligned with what I value for my future.

THE PERSONAL ACCOUNTABILITY CODE™

Step 3: Who Are You?

3. REFLECTION

Purpose of This Chapter

In the new science of accountability, there is infinitely greater chance of being accountable for successful goal achievement if you optimise your environment to leverage your preferences and strengths. This chapter is about setting up your goal-achieving environment for maximum success by understanding and using your innate personal drives, preferences and strengths to your greatest advantage. You will also consider the compelling consequences that motivate you as incentives and explore how you can organise your work environment for maximum satisfaction and minimum stress.

Even successful goal achievers experience blind spots regarding their strengths and areas for development that others see more clearly. This is why the art of asking for feedback is an important part of reflecting on the key question of this chapter: Who are you?

Chapter Exercises:

- Optimising Your Environment—What Drives You?
- Optimising Your Environment—The Work Styles Assessment
- Optimising Your Environment—What Motivates You?
- Optimising Your Environment—Know Your Strengths
- The Truth About Self-Discipline
- The Art of Asking for Feedback
- Checklist for Chapter 3

Optimising Your Environment for Success

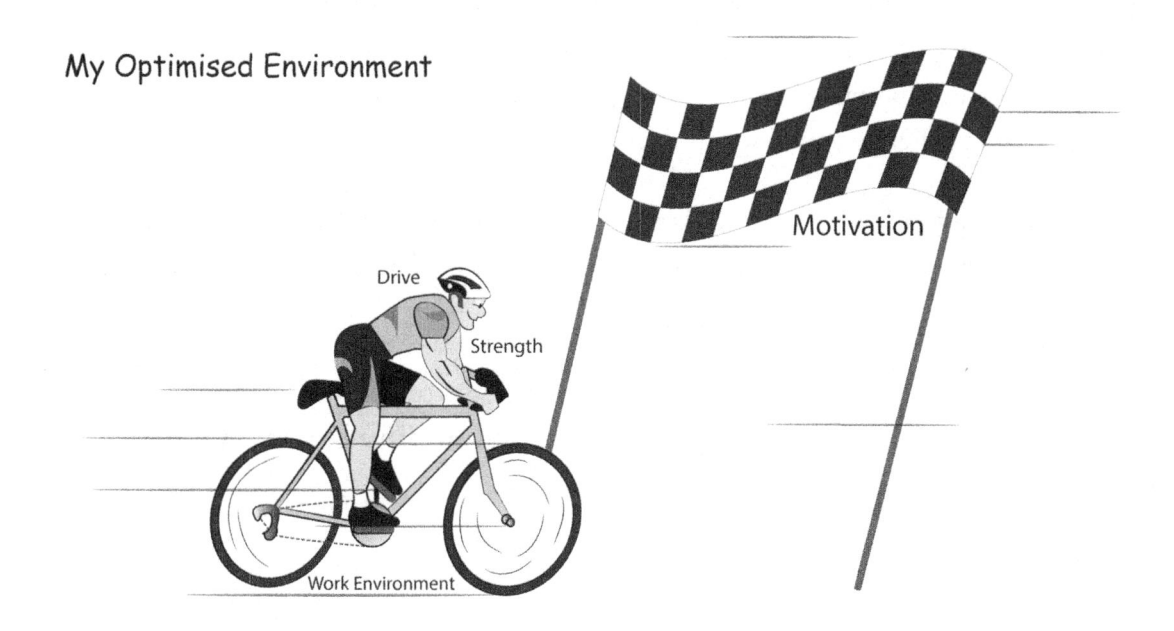

My Optimised Environment

(Illustration: a cyclist labeled with "Drive", "Strength", and "Work Environment" riding toward a checkered flag labeled "Motivation")

Optimising Your Environment—What Drives You?

I expect you already have a good idea of what drives you to action. You may have taken psychometric assessments and this would be a good time to review these. Record the results of previous assessments you have taken on personal characteristics such as:

- Your interests e.g. Strong Interest Inventory (SII), MAPP Career Assessment
- Your personality e.g. Myers Briggs Type Indicator (MBTI), Behavioural Style DISC Profile
- Your aptitude e.g. Clifton Strengths Finder 2.0, Values In Action (VIA)
- Your work and team preferences e.g. Team Management Profile (TMP), FIRO B
- Your leadership style e.g. The Leadership Practices Inventory (LPI), The Marshall Goldsmith Global Leader of the Future Inventory (GLOF)

I suggest you can always learn more about what drives you, both intrinsically and extrinsically. It is important to align your goals with your strongest drives. That way, you will set goals that come from a strong place of personal integrity. These goals are more likely to be more realistic, attainable and energising, and you will try to stretch yourself with those goals that will challenge you to grow.

Personal profiling and assessment tools are one way to understand what drives you. Another way is to look at what you've achieved over the years and what drove you to complete these goals and achievements.

Maybe it was a desire to feel powerful. Or perhaps it was to acquire things for your family. Or perhaps it was to help other people. Or maybe you are driven to simply learn and build your knowledge.

Extrinsic vs. Intrinsic Motivation

Extrinsic motivation is when you're offered a prize, a pay cheque or an incentive to complete a task; it's external.

Intrinsic motivation is internally driven: you'd do something without being rewarded, even if it means suffering or sacrifice. The reward is that kick of dopamine in the brain: it just feels good!

Start to develop your *self-awareness antennae*: when you catch yourself feeling motivated, reflect as to whether it is internal or external. Learn about yourself.

Anytime you struggle and overcome obstacles, it's because you have a strong drive to have, do or become something. The key is to identify what that is. It's a powerful source of energy.

That source of energy is different for everybody; for example, people work hard to get through college, but the reasons they do so are different. For some, it's to learn; for others,

STEP 3: WHO ARE YOU?

it's to get a job and earn money to acquire things; for others it's to achieve status or seek parental approval. Others do it for social reasons.

In the space below, make a list of two or three of your major achievements. Then record what drove you to pursue those goals. It can be anything: love, money, status, service, winning, or maybe just fun. But make a list of those things that light a fire for you and get your engines revved up.

What Drives Me...

Achievement 1
_____

What motivated me
_____

Achievement 2
_____

What motivated me
_____

Achievement 3
_____

What motivated me
_____

Now reflect on the list you just made about your achievements and what was driving you. Does anything appear more than once on the list? In the space below, summarise those things that drive and motivate you and rank in order of how strong they are, starting at number 1 as your greatest source of natural energy and drive.

Optimising Your Environment—The Work Styles Self-Assessment

To help you optimise your environment for successful goal achievement, the ideal is for your work environment to be organised to align with your personality, communication and work-style preferences where possible. *Work* could mean paid employment, or other (unpaid) tasks you undertake in order to achieve your goals.

Just as people choose what to wear from a variety of clothing styles, so people choose from a variety of behaviours that are situationally dependent. We act according to what our priorities are in that situation. Yet, we all have a preference for one way of acting over others.

Complete the exercise in this next section, which is a simple tool to help you identify the ways in which you prefer to respond to work demands.

Step 3: Who Are You?

Consider the following diagram:

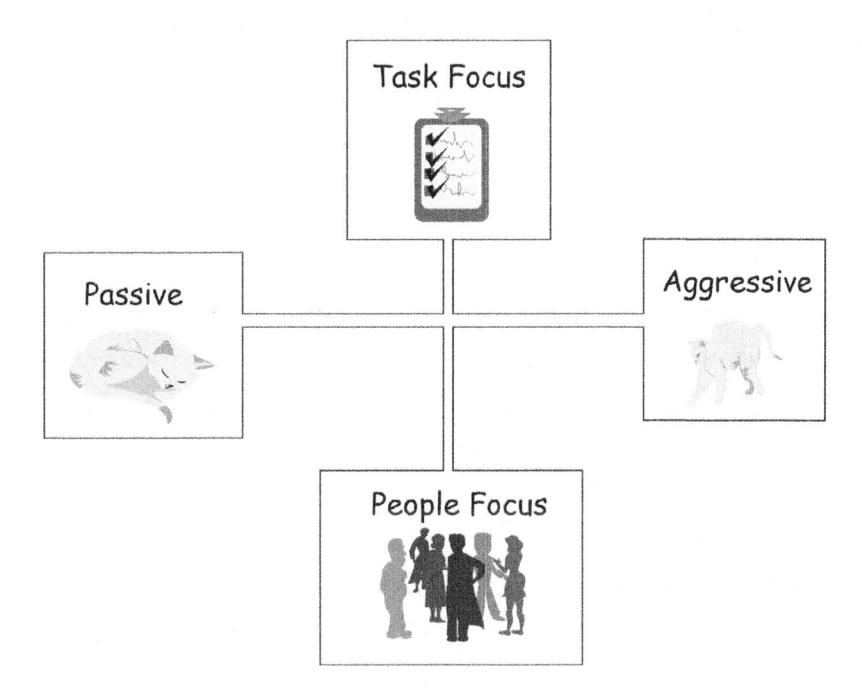

As I'm sure you've noticed, we all have habitual ways of approaching our work and other goal-achieving demands. Along the horizontal continuum, people tend to gravitate either to the passive or to the aggressive ends of the spectrum[3].

Where on the Passive—Assertive—Aggressive spectrum do you feel you tend to function?

- Passive
- Passive/Assertive
- Assertive
- Assertive/Aggressive
- Aggressive

---

3 A Climate for Change (2009) by Di Worrall

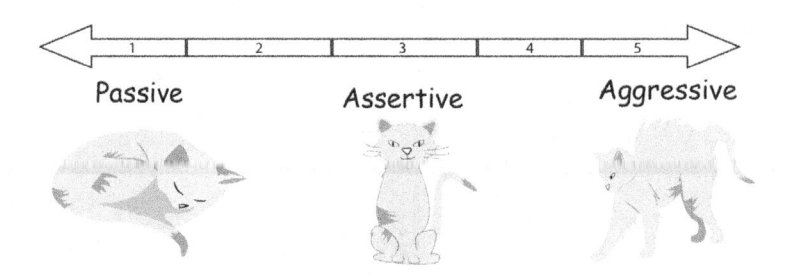

Where you sit on the spectrum can play a significant part in your capacity to achieve your goals and hold others accountable. The ideal is somewhere around the assertive centre. Too passive, and you risk sending mixed messages which are potentially hesitant, apologetic, self-deprecating and difficult for a listener to decipher. Conversely, you might tend too far into the aggressive end of the spectrum. In which case you might very well see people delivering results. However those results are likely to be short term, arising from fear and intimidation instead of genuine agreement to pursue a result. Discretionary effort and creativity all but go out the window.

Here are some tips for the passive or aggressive extremists next time you are striving to achieve your goals or hold someone accountable:

- To move from passive to more assertive behaviour:
  - Use "I" statements to let others know how you are thinking and feeling
  - Acknowledge the other person's feelings
  - Practice being assertive in front of a mirror for an upcoming situation—what you want to say, your posture and hand gestures
  - Rehearse saying "no" with confidence
  - If you are getting nowhere in a conversation, repeat your position in several different ways
  - Admit your mistakes
  - Ask whether you have an agreement
  - Clarify what you each understand the agreement is
  - Be specific about the next steps

- To move from aggressive to more assertive behaviour:
  - Listen more than talk
  - Ask what people think and respect their opinion
  - Use specific facts, behaviours and "I" statements to present your case instead of exaggerations and opinions
  - Avoid behaviour that is physically intimidating or bullying
  - Talk through objections
  - Admit your mistakes
  - Ask whether you have an agreement
  - Clarify what you each understand the agreement is
  - Be specific about the next steps

Along the vertical continuum of the diagram, some people tend to prioritise tasks and focus on getting things done. Others focus on people and pay more attention to feelings and relationships. Which do you tend towards at work?

☐ Tasks

Why? _____

or

☐ People?

Why? _____

The more you are aware of your natural tendencies, the better you'll be able to set priorities, schedule tasks and meetings, and take care of both the people and task aspects of your roles. Importantly, the more your work is aligned with your natural preferences, the less stress you will experience—and potentially greater happiness, fulfilment and personal satisfaction.

Now turn your attention to the vertical continuum and how you habitually approach tasks and relationships.

The Personal Accountability Code

Of course, reality tells us that people and tasks are not mutually exclusive and we need to focus on both at one time or another to fulfil our goals and responsibilities.

So let's take our analysis of the vertical column to a new level. You will see by the diagram that both the task and people orientations can further be analysed in terms of the purpose or an intention someone is trying to fulfil. There are four general intentions of every conversation and interaction:

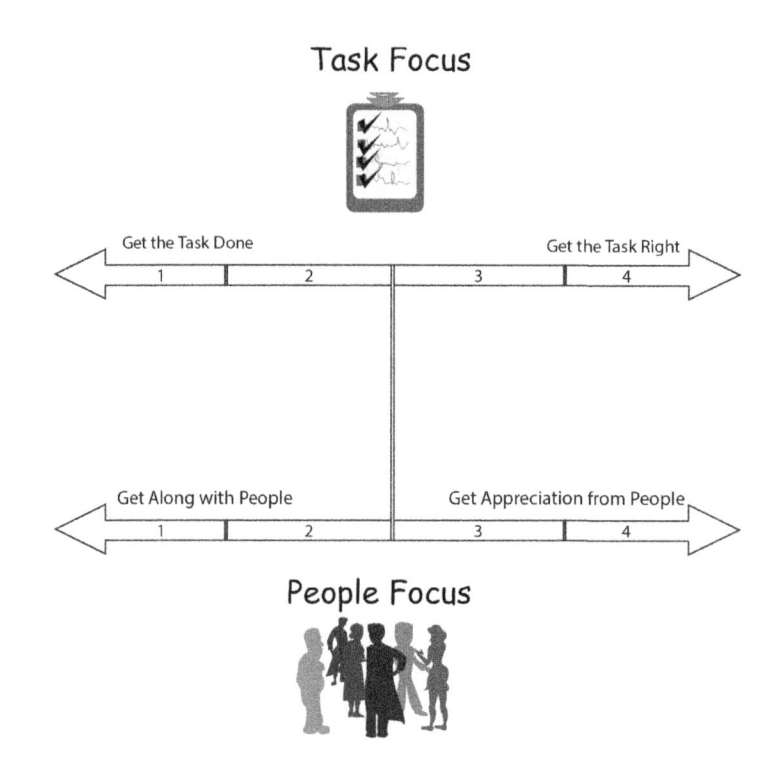

Task Focus

⇐ Get the Task Done | 1 | 2 | 3 | 4 | Get the Task Right ⇒

⇐ Get Along with People | 1 | 2 | 3 | 4 | Get Appreciation from People ⇒

People Focus

When we focus on a task, we either tend to get the task done or get the task right.

When we focus on people, our behaviour can either tend to enable us to get along with people or to get appreciation and respect from people.

In the following table, record how you typically approach each of these four intentions in order to fulfil your daily tasks and interactions with others. Often, it is dependent on the particular situation, but you know yourself well enough to be able to see your preference under normal conditions.

Step 3: Who Are You?

If you want a second opinion, ask a co-worker or trusted peer for their perspective.

Check the box by ranking your work preferences from 1 to 4, where:

1 = Definitely my priority *3. = Rarely a priority with me*
2 = Sometimes important to me *4. = Never a priority with me*

In my work environment, do I prefer to:	1	2	3	4
Get the task done? e.g., I prefer to schedule my workload so I can complete my assigned tasks in accordance with a system or deadline.				
Get the task right? e.g., I prefer to approach my work by creating something of quality with sufficient detail that I can be proud of. I would prefer not to be unduly pressured by deadlines if they compromise what I am doing.				
Get along with people? e.g., I am motivated more by social relationships at work than by status or the need for recognition. I would feel very uncomfortable doing something that would be an unpopular decision or would adversely affect people				
Get appreciated by people? e.g., I am more motivated by achieving appreciation and respect of people than being popular. Being respected sometimes means that I have to take hard decisions from time to time that may be unpopular,				

Answer the following questions on how you can use these insights about your habitual work style to organise your work environment for greater fulfilment, happiness and success. For example, if you scored 1 or 2 on any of the above, write down how you could create more opportunities to arrange the people or tasks in your environment to take advantage of your natural energy and drive.

The **Personal** Accountability Code

If you scored 3 or 4 on any of the above, write down an example of when this occurs in your working environment.

On a score of 1-5, how much stress and tension do you experience when these interactions are required of you at work, where 1 is very stressed and 5 is no stress?

The following are a few suggestions to consider if you are experiencing high levels of stress due to these interactions

- Seek out the support of a coach who can help you improve your stress management skills.
- Rearrange your work schedule, tasks or individual interactions (where possible) to realign your work arrangements so as to reduce your levels of stress and increase your focus and energy (this might mean keeping your day job, but adding more leisure activities to your schedule that motivate and inspire you)
- If your stress levels are over the top for you, you are not alone. Consider seeking the support of a trained medical health professional

If you are experiencing stress of 3 or more in the previous question, is this a level you want to reduce? If so, what actions do you intend to take?

Unless you live in a bubble, you are unlikely to be able to create an artificial environment which is 100% aligned with your view of the world—and I wouldn't suggest that to do so is particularly useful. In reality, even though we may have certain preferences, the necessities of life and work mean that we all display a rich and diverse tapestry of behaviours which fall into any and all preferences from time to time. It is also true that we can develop remarkably strong competency and career progression working out of preference, given the right environment.

No one style is right or wrong—just different. Everyone brings their own unique perspective and value to the table. The more you seek to understand how other people's strengths and preferences differ from yours, the greater your capacity to appreciate and leverage the contributions they can make to your goals.

Next time you find yourself stressed out by someone else's approach or view, take the time to enquire about their motivations, instead of making assumptions about their intentions. Enquiry is a vastly underutilised yet powerful tool you have at your disposal to connect with others who are instrumental to the achievement of your goals.

Optimising Your Environment—What Motivates You?

What sorts of things are appealing to you as compelling consequences and motivating rewards—the payoffs for putting in the hard yards—that contribute to your personal motivation, contentment, satisfaction and self-esteem? Examine the following examples for different areas of your life and see what resonates with you. Be honest with yourself here. Not all motivations have to be high and mighty, and some are inherent in the experience itself. What motivates you is likely to be quite different from what motivates someone else; for example, you might enjoy getting recognised for good work—others may hate it. A very important point to be aware of if you are attempting to motivate someone else towards goal achievements.

Motivators in Your Environment: Time of day or night; certain locations; specific people; sounds or silence.

Motivators for your Health & Fitness: Looking good in your favourite outfit; feeling stronger; feeling more competitive; hitting that number on the scales; feeling more attractive.

Motivators in your Work and Career: Getting recognised for good work; money; career advancement; winning; the game/competition; being part of the team; receiving special privileges or bonuses; the feeling of 'power' and control; sense of security; the personal satisfaction of achievement; the joy of being 'in flow'; the belief you've made a difference; the experience of being of service.

Motivators in your Finances: Security; financial freedom; purchasing what I want; living the lifestyle I desire; satisfaction of being debt-free.

Motivators in your Family and Relationships: Giving love and attention; receiving love and attention; a happy family; a healthy family; family achievements; pride; happiness.

Motivators in your Community: Recognition; the personal satisfaction of contributing to a higher good; seeing what you do impacting the community; progress within your community; helping others; seeing others benefit from your contributions, being the quiet achiever.

Motivators in your Spiritual Life: Feeling closer to your creator; peace; joy; love, feeling grateful.

Motivators in your Leisure Activities: Relaxation; excitement; happiness; achievement; competition; feeling of 'flow'.

The point is to identify what works for you for each area in your life. Make a list of your strongest, most compelling rewards.

___

___

___

Optimising Your Environment—Know Your Strengths

Besides knowing what drives you, it's important to know what you're good at. There's a considerable amount of research showing that people are more successful when they place more focus on improving their strengths instead of expending all their effort in trying to overcome their weaknesses.

Most people place a great deal of emphasis on overcoming their faults or deficiencies. But they either don't make much progress, or the path is just too hard, so they abandon their efforts. Instead, the new science of accountability indicates there is great value in placing as much effort as possible into improving what we're already naturally inclined to accomplish.

Step 3: Who Are You?

It makes no sense to channel efforts into a losing battle—but we're programmed from an early age to focus on what's wrong. We'd be wiser to also focus sufficient time and attention on our strengths. When you make progress and improve what you're already good at, you generate positive self-esteem and energy for even more progress, giving you a stronger anchor to see you through the times when you need to face up to things you're not so good at.

Your strengths are defined by your actual activities. They are things you do consistently and with some effort, near perfectly. They might be in your innate gifts, such as your memory, body type, sense of direction, creativity, character, personality type or work orientation. They might appear as the skills and knowledge you have developed over time, such as in music, mathematics, writing, analysis, entrepreneurship or a trade. Or they may appear as a composite of your unique life experiences; e.g., courage in the face of adversity, leadership, parenthood, entrepreneurial achievements, community/voluntary contributions.

You can identify your strengths by the acronym **SIGN**:

- **S** = Something that you have easy **Success** with
- **I** = **Instinctively** are drawn to
- **G** = You use it frequently and naturally **Grow** from it
- **N** = It seems to fill an internal **Need**

To be brief, your strengths are those activities that make you feel strong. Use this list to help identify what you consider as your top five strengths and why. *(Hint: Record your top five strengths and why in your online Personal Accountability Code™ Report.)*

1. _____
2. _____
3. _____
4. _____
5. _____

Other people can recognise strengths that you might not see in yourself. Ask your coach or accountability partner to also identify what they see as your top five strengths and why.

THE **PERSONAL** ACCOUNTABILITY CODE

1. _____
2. _____
3. _____
4. _____
5. _____

The Truth About Self-Discipline

It often seems that self-discipline comes easiest when we are engaging in a task which we naturally enjoy and which is aligned with our motivations, talents and strengths. It also seems to follow that self-discipline can be a burden when it is in relation to tasks that we don't find as enjoyable. While this is often the case, it doesn't have to be.

In truth, self-discipline can be equally applied to any task when we uncover the reward underpinning that task—whether it is our preference or not. It is also likely that you have already developed this skill somewhere in your life. You wash the dishes—not because you enjoy washing dishes, but because you enjoy having a clean and clear kitchen. You pursue several subjects you don't enjoy in amongst those you do in a course of study—not because you want to study subjects you don't enjoy, but because the payoff of a higher degree and employment opportunities is so compelling.

In each and every task, there is always a payoff—a reward, a higher purpose for doing something. Find the reward and you will find your path of least resistance.

Think of an example where you are quite easily self-disciplined in a task you don't enjoy. What is the payoff for completing this task?

_____
_____

Know How to Ask for Feedback

We all have blind spots and don't know it—that's precisely why they're called blind spots. These can be both positive and negative.

It can be a lot easier to see some qualities in others than it is to see them in ourselves. We are quite adept at fooling ourselves, but those issues may be very obvious to the people observing us. This can hold true for even the most successful among us.

We have an opportunity to learn more about ourselves when we stop, ask, listen and think about feedback from others. But there's a right way to ask for feedback, and many wrong ways as well.

One of the world's leading coaches, Marshall Goldsmith, voted #1 leadership thinker in the world (*Harvard Business Review*) offers a great suggestion about soliciting feedback from others in order to grow. Here's what he has to say:

> *'In my experience, there are a hundred wrong ways to ask for feedback—and one right way. Most of us know the wrong ways. We ask someone:*
> - *What do you think of me? (How do you feel about me?)*
> - *What do you hate about me?*
> - *What do you like about me?'*

Why are the above phrases wrong? Because they set both you and the giver of the feedback up for hurt feelings and a damaged relationship. They tend to focus on things that are inherent to you or your character that you may not be in a position to change and hence are left feeling powerless and deflated.

The Right Question to Ask: How Can I Do Better?

Dr Goldsmith explains that seeking out issue-free feedback by asking, '*How Can I Do Better?*' makes change possible because it:

1. Solicits advice rather than criticism.
2. Is directed towards the future rather than negative things that have happened in the past.
3. Is couched in a way that suggests you will act on it; that in fact you are trying to get better.

The Feedforward Exercise

Practise this valuable skill now. Select an area of your life you would like to focus on.

My focus area: _____

Ask your coach, a trusted colleague or accountability partner for some suggestions as to '*How Can I Do Better?*' and record their answer. Make a point of receiving their suggestions with grace and thanks, without judgement, discussion, justification or argument. Simply saying 'thank you' is the best way to acknowledge their contribution. That way they are more likely to feel valued and appreciated, and you keep the communication channels open for next time.

Feedforward Notes:

_____
_____
_____
_____
_____
_____
_____

STEP 3: WHO ARE YOU?

After you leave the conversation, find a private space and record whether you intend to proceed with any of their suggestions.

This now completes Step 3 of your *Personal Accountability Code*™. Congratulations!

Checklist for Chapter 3—Who Am I?

- ☐ I have a good idea about **what drives me to action**, having reviewed my prior personality and preference assessments where applicable
- ☐ I have reviewed **how I can optimise my work environment** for successful goal achievement
- ☐ I understand what appeals to me as **compelling consequences and motivating** rewards
- ☐ I have a good understanding of **my strengths**.
- ☐ I understand more about how I can apply the process of **self-discipline** to important tasks
- ☐ I know how to **ask others for feedback using the feedforward technique** so I can learn more about myself.

THE PERSONAL ACCOUNTABILITY CODE™

Step 4: Where Are You Now?

THE **PERSONAL** ACCOUNTABILITY CODE

Purpose of This Chapter

This chapter of the *Personal Accountability Code*™ addresses the question: *Where are you now vs. Where do you want to be?*

In this chapter, you'll take your vision to the next level. As you work your way through the exercises, you will take stock of *where you are now* in relation to the vision *of where you want to go* that you identified in Chapter 2.

In the new science of accountability, much can be learned about personal goal achievement from the fields of business planning and analysis. If you were to apply business planning terminology to this exercise, you'd be analysing your personal current-state assessment in relation to your ideal future state. The challenge then becomes how you close the gap between the two. The steps you decide to take in closing this gap become the foundations of your Personal Accountability Plan.

In this chapter, you will take the vision you crafted in Chapter 2 and break it down into a number of more detailed dimensions using the Wheel of Life tool. You will examine where you are right now in relation to where you want to be across several specific dimensions of your life. Then you'll then take a comprehensive look at the resources that are available to you, what stands in the way of your vision of the future, and what you need to have or do to get where you want to go.

Exercises:

- The Wheel of Life
- SPOT Analysis (Internal Strengths, Internal Problems, External Opportunities, External Threats)
- Strengths—Problems Gap Analysis
- Opportunities—Threats Gap Analysis
- The Truth About Habits
- Checklist for Chapter 4

STEP 4: WHERE ARE YOU NOW?

The Wheel of Life

In Chapter 2, you created a vision of your ideal future. Now it's time to drill down into the detail, and create the means to achieve your vision across several specific life dimensions.

Fill in each segment of the pie with the major dimensions of interest or roles in your life. You can either fill them all in or choose the categories most relevant to you at this time. For example:

1. Personal development
2. Work, career, business
3. Relationships, family, children
4. Leisure, Sports, hobbies, fun
5. Friends, community involvement, charities
6. Physical well-being, fitness, health, nutrition
7. Spiritual or philosophical interests
8. Finances, savings, debt
9. Physical environment, home
10. Other…

(It doesn't matter how many 'pieces of the pie' your wheel has; it's important to identify the areas in your life that are important to *you*.)

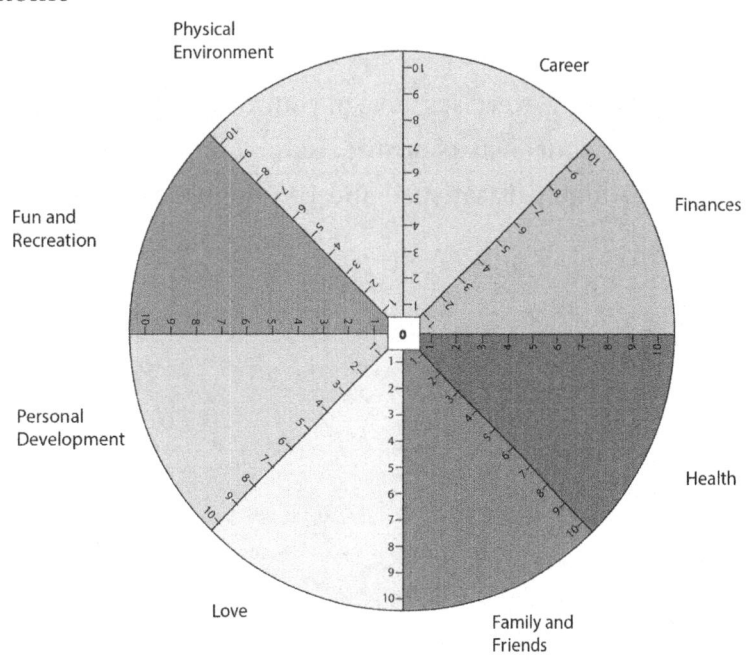

The **Personal** Accountability Code

In the following example, the *fun and recreation* dimension of life is rated as highly dissatisfying and is shaded as no more than 2/10. In contrast, the *career* dimension is rated as highly satisfying, with shading at 8/10.

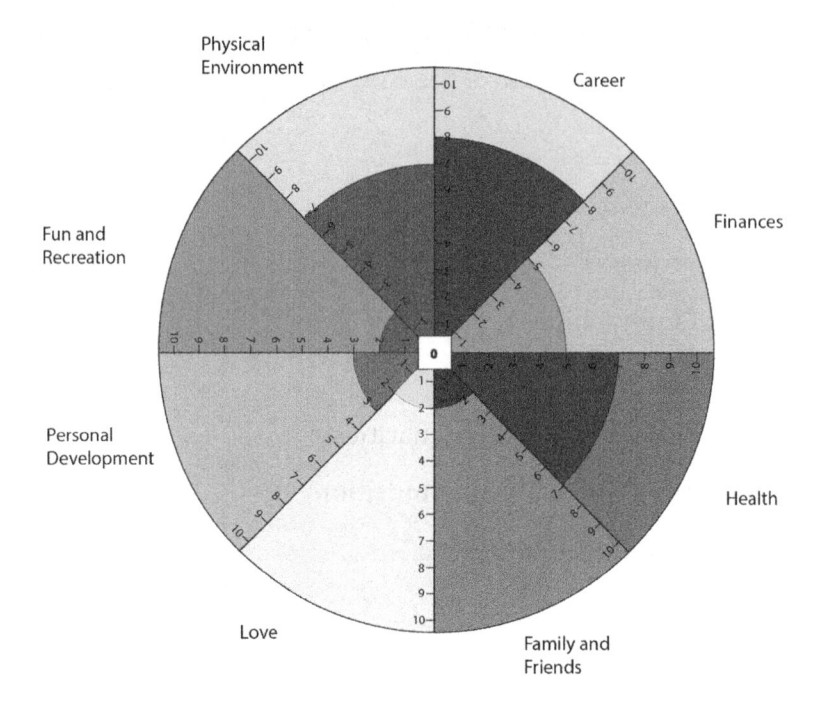

In the following exercises, design your own Wheel of Life using the suggested dimensions or some of your own choosing. Rate your level of satisfaction in each piece of the pie, where 1 is highly dissatisfied and 10 is highly satisfied.

STEP 4: WHERE ARE YOU NOW?

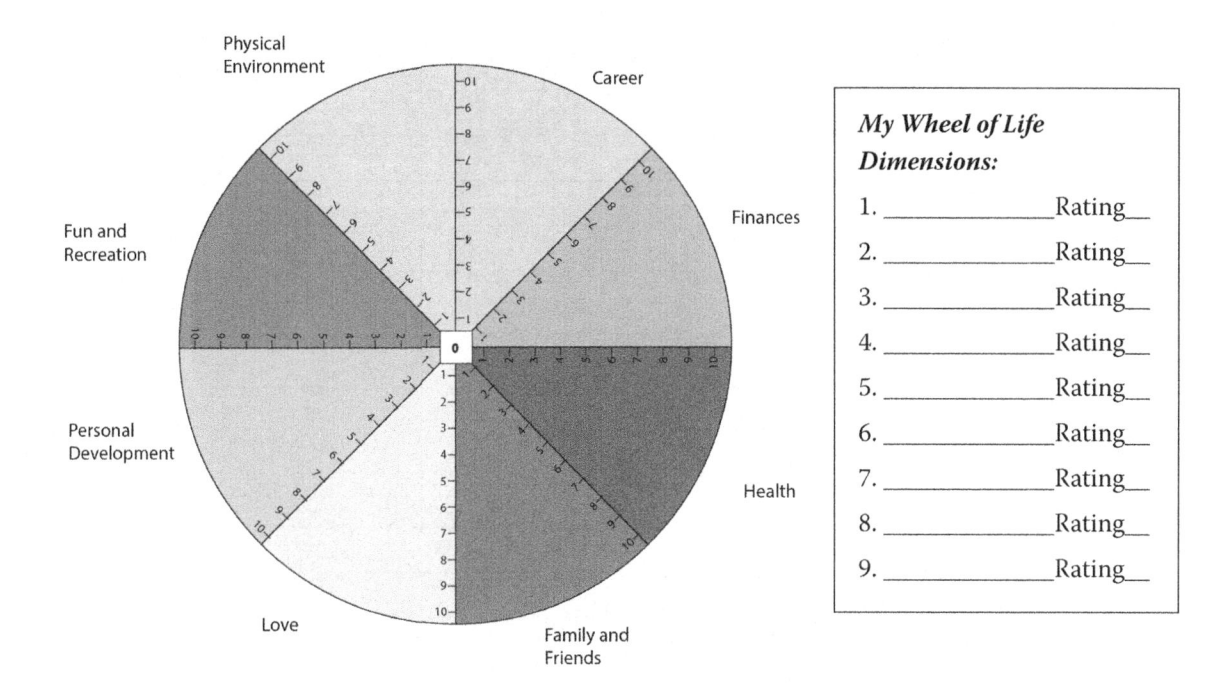

My Wheel of Life Dimensions:

1. _____Rating__
2. _____Rating__
3. _____Rating__
4. _____Rating__
5. _____Rating__
6. _____Rating__
7. _____Rating__
8. _____Rating__
9. _____Rating__

Prioritise your list by selecting up to five dimensions of your Wheel of Life that are at the top of your agenda for personal change over the next 12 months, and answer the following questions. (The dimensions may be dissatisfying—or the dimension could be most satisfying, yet you want to strive for even more. The choice is yours.)

Dimension 1: _____

❒ Why change?

The **Personal** Accountability Code

☐ Why change now?

___

Dimension 2: ___

☐ Why change?

___

☐ Why change now?

___

Dimension 3: ___

☐ Why change?

___

Step 4: Where Are You Now?

☐ Why change now?

_____
_____
_____
_____
_____

Dimension 4: _____

☐ Why change?

_____
_____
_____
_____
_____

☐ Why change now?

_____
_____
_____
_____
_____

Dimension 5: _____

☐ Why change?

_____
_____
_____
_____
_____

THE **PERSONAL** ACCOUNTABILITY CODE

☐ Why change now?

_____
_____
_____
_____
_____

SPOT Analysis

Another important element of your personal current state analysis is to conduct an honest examination of your strengths and talents along with the environment in which you live and work. There are four areas to define in the 'SPOT' quadrants:

- Strengths—the talent or resources I have
- Problems—the talent or resources I need
- Opportunities—to be leveraged in my environment
- Threats—to be mitigated or eliminated in my environment

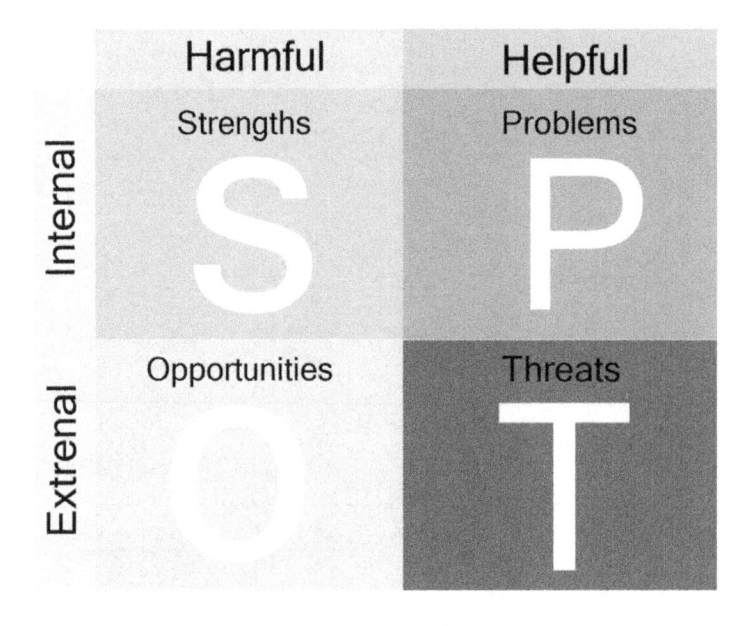

	Harmful	Helpful
Internal	Strengths **S**	Problems **P**
Extrenal	Opportunities **O**	Threats **T**

By the end of this section, you will be another important step closer to achieving your goals because you will know:

1. How to leverage the 'sweet spot' of your current strengths and opportunities in your environment
2. How to either mitigate or eliminate the 'sour spot' where your personal talents and resources and environmental threats present obstacles to your achieving your goals for change

Strengths

What do you have or do that helps you to be successful?

- ❒ What are your personal and professional strengths? (NB: You can refer to things such as your responsibility-readiness assessment, personal accountability index, psychometric assessments, work-style assessment, skills, experience, credentials, networks, customer relationships, value you add, your strengths assessment, drives and motivation)

_____
_____
_____
_____
_____
_____
_____
_____
_____
_____
_____
_____
_____
_____

The Personal Accountability Code

☐ What resources are available to you that can help your achieve your intentions for change—people, tools, equipment, money, assets.

Problems

What obstacles are standing in the way of your achieving what you want?

☐ What don't you have that you need to successfully achieve what's important?

☐ What can't you do as well as you could, that stands in the way of your success? (NB: refer to resources such as your responsibility-readiness assessment, personal accountability index, psychometric assessment, drives and motivation, work-style assessment, skills inventory.)

The Limitations of a Fixed Mindset

In the previous exercise on 'Problems', I asked that you consider '*What can't you do **as well as you could**, that stands in the way of your success?*' Note the phrase '*as well as you could*. I did not suggest outright that you **can't** do something. The fact that you are unable do something well **right now** doesn't have to define who you are forever—unless you allow it to.

Just because in some situations you procrastinate, for example, doesn't mean you have to define yourself as a 'procrastinator'. Just because you prefer the order of facts and figures to the less structured realm of creative thought doesn't mean you are not 'creative'. Just because you didn't learn to use an iPad before you could walk doesn't mean that you are 'technically challenged' when it comes to modern technology. Just because you have been unable to quit smoking as yet doesn't mean that you are a 'smoker' forever. It's just that you haven't found the way to quit that works for you.

Digging our heels in and holding on to a fixed mindset about what we think we *can't* do can significantly limit our capacity to grow, learn and see the opportunity do something differently.

Review your answers to the last exercise that asked the question *'What can't you do as well as you could, that stands in the way of your success?'* Is there anything in your answer that might suggest you may be limiting your opportunities for success with a fixed mindset about what you can't do—instead of how things could be?

Now take your insights from this question and the exercises on strengths and problems into the next section, on Gap Analysis.

Gap Analysis

Based on your assessments of your strengths and problem areas (having regard to the limitations of a fixed mindset), identify where there are gaps between what you have (strengths) and what you need (problems) to achieve your intentions for change—for example:

- **Health & Fitness:** I want to drop 1-0 kg. I have the desire, the money and the time. The gap is lack of willpower and absence of a structured system of healthy eating and fitness.
- **Career:** I aspire to win my first team leader appointment. I have a good employee track record and experience as a leader of projects, as well as the desire to move to the next level. The gap is absence of formal team leader training, poor commercial acumen, and a career plan.

Step 4: Where Are You Now?

How will you specifically close these gaps—e.g., pursue a specific personal/professional development goal, secure resources? (You will convert these gaps into specific goals and action steps in Chapter 5 of your *Personal Accountability Code*™.)

THE **PERSONAL** ACCOUNTABILITY CODE

Opportunities (in Your Environment)

- ☐ What could you take advantage of in your personal or work environment that would help you achieve your vision for change (job vacancy, new project, new study semester, peer support, mastermind group, study group, social media)?

_____
_____
_____
_____
_____
_____
_____
_____
_____
_____

- ☐ How can you build these opportunities into your accountability action plan?

_____
_____
_____
_____
_____
_____
_____
_____

Threats (in Your Environment)

☐ What are the external circumstances that may undermine your success in achieving your vision for change (e.g., organisational restructuring, job under threat, unsupportive boss, rising interest rates, negative family and friends)?

_____
_____
_____
_____
_____
_____
_____
_____
_____
_____
_____
_____

☐ How will you address these threats or any obstacles in your action plan? (The way you intend to manage these risks will become action steps in your Personal Accountability Action Plan.)

_____
_____
_____

The Truth About Habits

Any attempt to change something in our lives is bound to come face to face with a barrage of unconscious routines and habits that we have acquired through the years. Some of those routines will support the changes we want; others are likely to undermine them. It may be that one of your reasons for working through *The Personal Accountability Code*™ is that you want to change a habit; e.g., overeating, smoking, not exercising, biting your nails, getting angry.

Have you heard the story that it takes 21 days to form a new habit? Sorry to burst your bubble, but that's all it is—a good story. In truth, there is little research to support that theory. The reality is that forming new habits is a little more challenging. But the good news is that it's entirely possible.

Step 4: Where Are You Now?

Charles Duhigg, in his 2012 book *The Power of Habit,* offers some interesting insights on the latest research on forming new habits. In order to develop a new habit, you'll need to understand the anatomy of a habit.

- Habits are triggered by a cue
- The cue triggers a habitual unconscious routine
- Performing that routine gives us a reward

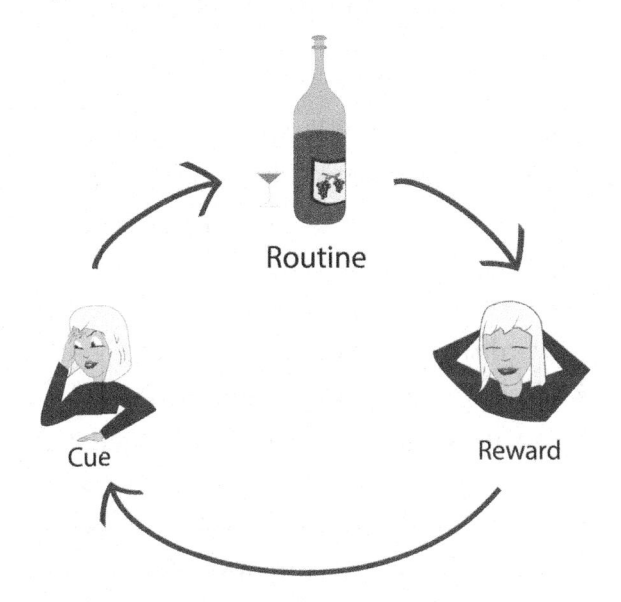

Given this background as to how habits work, we can see that we will be more effective in breaking a habit we don't want if we actually strive to replace it by something else. It is important to actually keep the *cue* and the *reward* in place. The steps for replacing an old habit with a new one are to:

1. Select the habit you want to replace
2. Uncover the cue that sets your habit in motion
3. Identify the payoff/reward you experience that is attached to the habit you want to change
4. Link the same cue and the same reward to a different habit/routine (or change your environment and get rid of the temptation of the cue altogether—but realise that the habit will still be there)

5. Underpin that new habit with a belief that change is possible
6. Connect with another person/accountability partner or coach who shares that belief and is willing to help reinforce your new routine. The experience of change becomes real when you can see the reflection of your new habits in someone else's perception of you.

A friend of mine, Kylie, was happy to share the following story of how she used this process to successfully break a daily habit she had developed of drinking several glasses of wine every evening.

Kylie's cue to this daily habit turned out to be quite a complex routine. She would finish her day at work, arrive home, remove her jewellery and make-up, take a shower and get into her relaxing 'home clothes'. She would head straight for the kitchen, reach for a wine glass, grab a bottle of wine and then fill the glass.

I asked Kylie about the reward she was experiencing at the conclusion of this ritual. She described the reward as a feeling that she experienced as the glass was filled. 'I am calm. It's family time,' she said. 'Whatever goes on now I can handle. I am rattled by nothing.'

We tested this feeling, and it appeared that it kicked in once the glass was filled and before she did anything else. Where she drank the wine was not particularly important.

Within this complex ritual, the specific habit that Kylie wanted to replace was drinking the wine, as it was beginning to pile on the kilos.

Kylie decided to replace the wine with a hot cup of green tea, in the belief that it was possible to replace the wine-drinking habit. Most of the ritual surrounding this habit remained the same—but instead of reaching for a wine glass and wine bottle, she reached for a tea cup and kettle to fill a cup of tea. She also moved the kettle into a more prominent position for easy access.

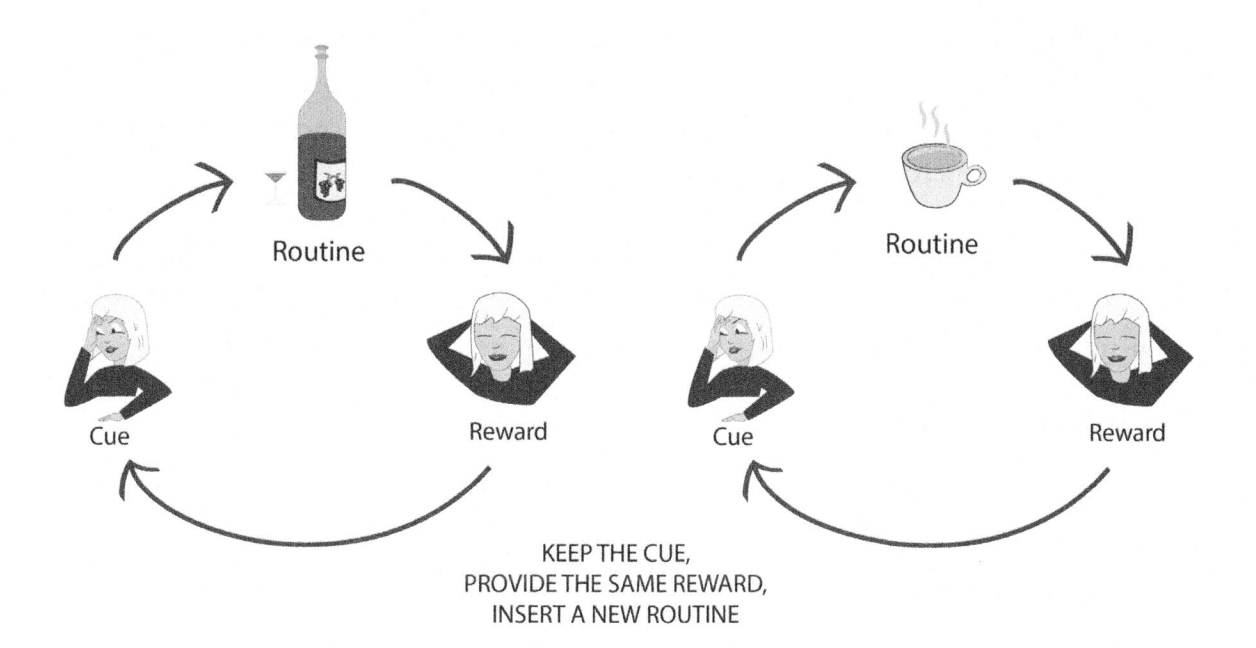

**KEEP THE CUE,
PROVIDE THE SAME REWARD,
INSERT A NEW ROUTINE**

This new sequence worked. Kylie felt satisfied just by holding the cup of tea in her hand—before even taking the first sip. Further, she felt neither the specific need to hold a wine glass nor a craving for wine. It turned out that the feelings of satisfaction and calm were triggered by retaining the same after-work ritual, followed by making herself something (anything) to drink.

The new, healthier habit was reinforced by guilt-free feelings that those extra kilos began to easily fall away as a result of this simple change in one daily habit. Another important part of Kylie's reinforcement of this new habit was to share the challenge and success of the experience with her girlfriends—aka 'accountability partners'.

It would be easy to think that Kylie had a kind of obsessive-compulsive disorder, given the complexity of this ritual; however, the truth really is stranger than fiction. In reality, we all share thousands of seemingly bizarre rituals and habits just like Kylie's in our own lives. It's just that most of our rituals and habits occur on an unconscious level, so we don't particularly notice them.

If you have a habit that you want to change, it is probably embedded in a complex sequence of rituals like this. If you want to get a handle on a habit, grab a journal, find an accountability partner and start documenting exactly what happens around the habit you want to change, when it occurs, where and why. Experiment replacing the habit with something else. See what produces the same satisfying feelings. You might be surprised at what you find. You might even have some laughs along the way.

Not all of our intentions for change need to be great and lofty goals that will impact the world. Perhaps you just have a small, annoying habit that, if replaced, will improve your quality of life (or others') and allow you to focus on more important priorities.

How might your habits be helping or hindering progress towards your goals?

_____

Is there a habit you would like to change now? What is it?

_____

I can't tell you how long it will take to replace the particular habit you want to change. For a simple habit, try working through the above process using a private journal and sharing your experience with an accountability partner. I would, however, recommend that if you have a really stubborn or destructive habit that you want to get a handle on, you seek out the support of a trained therapist, psychologist, medical or other appropriately qualified professional.

> ## Checklist for Chapter 4—Where Am I Now?
>
> Here is a checklist for your current-state assessment—*Where you are now vs. Where you want to be*:
>
> - ☐ Using the **Wheel of Life**, I have identified the important dimensions of my life.
> - ☐ I have identified and prioritised **what I want to change** and why.
> - ☐ I have **completed my personal SPOT Analysis** and understand how I can leverage my personal strengths and the opportunities in my environment.
> - ☐ I have examined where I might be limiting my opportunities for success with a **fixed mindset** about what I can't do
> - ☐ I have reviewed the **risks of making changes**, so that I can either mitigate or eliminate the problems and threats to my goals.
> - ☐ I have read about the anatomy of **habits**, and identified how my habits could be helping or hindering my progress.

You really are making the most amazing progress! In the next chapter, you get down to the business of selecting your goals and creating an Action Plan for their achievement.

THE PERSONAL ACCOUNTABILITY CODE™

Step 5: How Are You Getting There?

5. PLANNING

THE **PERSONAL** ACCOUNTABILITY CODE

Purpose of This Chapter

Which priorities should you focus on to create a roadmap for change that is most likely to get you where you want to go? This chapter focuses on the art of goal setting and how the new science of accountability helps you succeed with goal completion.

You will create a powerful action plan for successful goal choice and completion, anchored to the familiar SMART goal-setting principles:

Specific—Measurable—Action-oriented—Realistic—Time-Bound

By the end of this chapter you will have an Accountability Action Plan that looks something like this:

My Accountability Action Plan

My Vision & Values Statement :

Wheel of Life Dimension	Specific Goals	Milestones	Action Steps	Reality Check	Time-frame
Health	I easily maintain a healthy weight range	I weigh x lbs by 1st December	Book appointment with doctor Establish weigh in targets Find an accountability partner	y y y	Next week Weekly 2 Weeks

However, by the end of this book, your Personal Accountability Action Plan will be even **SMART + ER**. In Chapter 6, we will bolster your plan with two new elements that give you the winner's edge for staying on track and accountable to your goals.

Specific—Measurable—Action-oriented—Realistic—Time-Bound
+ Energy + Reinforcement

This is the ultimate personal accountability action plan—that you are unlikely to wriggle out of as soon as something goes wrong—which it will!

Exercises:

The SMARTER 7-Step Process for Successful Goal Achievement

- Goal Achievement Step 1—Select **Specific** Goals
- Goal Achievement Step 2—Establish **Measures** of Success
- Goal Achievement Step 3—Determine **Action** Steps
- Goal Achievement Step 4—Be **Realistic**
- Goal Achievement Step 5—Align to a **Timeframe**
- Goal Achievement Step 6—Ensure goals are **Energising** (Chapter 6)
- Goal Achievement Step 7—**Reinforce** progress (Chapter 6)

Why Set Goals?

We humans seem to be naturally goal-seeking beings. Yet people vary immensely when it comes to their ability to accomplish goals.

For sure, those who master goal setting and achievement are more successful in life and career. They experience more life satisfaction than those who don't accomplish goals. The good news is that this is something *you* can learn to do.

Goals that are specific and deemed challenging to achieve tend to increase performance more than goals that are simple and vague. The key is in finding just the right degree of challenge. A goal that is too easy doesn't provide as much satisfaction as one that requires you to stretch yourself.

Benefits of Goal Setting

Setting goals will affect you in five ways:

1. **Choice**: Goals focus our attention and direct efforts to goal-relevant activities. This helps you minimise distractions from irrelevant actions. It keeps your energy channelled towards the activities that truly matter most.

2. **Focus**: Goal-directed behaviours build skills and knowledge where it counts. When you focus on a goal, you learn quickly and are able to create more effective habits.

3. **Effort**: Goals require effort. When you work intensely towards a goal, you get better at it. Tasks become easier with practice, allowing other stretch goals to be set.

4. **Persistence**: A person becomes more skilled at handling setbacks when pursuing a goal. You learn intensely when you work through obstacles to achieve success.

5. **Personal growth**: Goals lead you to develop and change your behaviour; therefore, you acquire new skills and learn along the way.

Of course, we rarely have a clean slate of non-conflicting goals. All human beings are complex and some of us 'want it all'. In chapter 6, we'll spend some time reviewing obstacles that get in the way of goal completion—because if you're not aware of them, you'll get caught in their traps.

Our brains are problem-solving, goal-achieving machines. Goals help us get what we want.

Characteristics of Effective Goals

Most goal-setting experts agree that, to be most effective, the best goals are SMART:

1. **Specific**: Goals are defined, specific and written down.
2. **Measurable**: Goals track progress so that forward movement can be acknowledged, obstacles can be noted and addressed, and goal completion is clearly evident when accomplished.

3. **Action oriented:** Goals are described in terms of the specific steps or tasks required to achieve them.
4. **Realistic**: Goals ideally involve a sufficient level of challenge to stretch beyond one's usual capacity, yet be attainable. Goals should have the right timing, can realistically be adequately resourced and obstacles overcome.
5. **Timeframe**: Goals should be tied to a deadline

In this workbook, we take the concept of **SMART** goals and make them **SMARTER**, ensuring they connect to the accountability framework you have progressively established in chapters 1 through 4 of this workbook.

SMARTER goals are also:

- **Energised** by leveraging your existing strengths to tap into the natural sources of positive energy and drive that are unique to you; and
- **Reinforced** using a powerful system to keep you on track, including positive, supportive review through feedback, and feedforward and follow-through, to carry you through the inevitable obstacles ahead and reward you as you celebrate your progress.

A Process for Successful Goal Achievement

Out of all the desires, wishes, ideal future, problems, and challenges you think about, which should you select to work on right now? Ideally, you want to pick something that will take you on the fastest, most direct path to where you want to go.

You may have a clearly defined roadmap for where you're going, or you may not. In either case, you can't go wrong using the SMARTER goal achievement process.

The **Personal** Accountability Code

Goal Achievement Step 1—Select Specific Goals

S	M	A	R	T	E	R
Select Specific Goals						

'It's a dream until you write it down, and then it's a goal.'

Unknown

Source Documents: Vision and Values, Strengths Analysis, Drives & Motivations, SPOT Analysis, The Wheel of Life

Instructions

In this exercise, you will select the goals that are most likely to close the gap in your SPOT Analysis between where you are and where you want to be. Using your most pressing Wheel of Life dimensions, you will refer to the source documents below and identify those goals that seem to be a best fit with your visions and values, strengths, drives and motivations.

- **The Wheel of Life**—Look at your Wheel of Life analysis from Chapter 4 and Select at least 5 dimensions to work on.

- **Vision and Values Statements**—Reflect on your vision and values statements when choosing the right goals to work on. You don't want to work hard at obtaining outcomes that aren't important to you.

- **Strengths Analysis**—Make sure what you're going after is anchored to at least one of your strengths. You can't expect to be successful if you try to become what you're not.

- **Drives and Motivations**—The goals you select must be inspiring and motivational so you are more likely to stick with them for the long haul.

  Here are some questions to ask yourself when deciding which goals to work on (from *Die Empty* by Todd Henry):

- What problems or complaints do you find yourself consistently gravitating towards?
- What do you see, hear, read or experience that provokes compassionate anger?
- What will you stand for today, that's worth the fight?
- **SPOT Analysis**—What gaps do you want to close between *where you are now* and *where you want to be*?

How to Choose the Right Goals

In the next section you will be filling in the Goal Selection template. Review the following guidelines and examples to assist you in the process of selecting the right goals.

Step 1

In The Personal Accountability Code™ Step 4, you identified up to 5 dimensions of your Wheel of Life that you feel motivated to take action on:

1. Personal development
2. Work, career, business
3. Relationships, family, children
4. Leisure, sports, hobbies, fun
5. Friends, community involvement, charities
6. Physical well-being, fitness, health, nutrition
7. Spiritual or philosophical interests
8. Finances, savings, debt
9. Physical environment, home
10. Other_____

Step 2

In relation to each of the 5 dimensions you selected from the Wheel of Life in Step 1, spend at least 5-10 minutes writing down as many goals as you can think of that will help you achieve more success in that domain.

Step 3
Review your list and bundle similar goals together.

Step 4
For each bundle of goals, mark it as either A, B, or C in order of importance, from the most important and realistic to the least important. If necessary, complete this prioritisation exercise again for your 'A' selections until you have no more than seven goals.

Step 5
Rewrite your final goal selections as statements in the positive present tense, as though they occurring right now. Why write goals in the present tense? Writing down a goal in the positive present tense might seem counter-intuitive for something that has not yet happened; however, there is a very good reason for writing out your goals and intentions as though they exist in your current reality.

There is a part of your subconscious brain known as the reticular activating system (RAS); this part of the brain operates to guide your focus, attention and arousal on matters associated with your current belief systems. What happens when you state a goal as something you 'will' achieve in the future is that you leave your reticular activating system with no choice but to act on the goal as something that is not relevant to its present belief system. It goes to work to diligently sabotage your efforts to go for your goal as this goal doesn't make sense in its present reality.

This is where many of your status quo muscles are hiding and actively conspiring to resist change in your life. If you want to break through this barrier to achieving your goals, it is important to 'trick' your RAS into thinking that you are in fact *living* your goal right now, by using phrases like 'I am' or 'I have' in your goal statements. That way, you insert a new belief 'program' into your brain that then goes to work in your subconscious to search for all the ways to ensure your new 'belief' system is congruent with your reality.

Step 6
Add a word that represents the feeling of what it is like to achieve the goal.

Step 7
Visualise in your mind's eye what it is like to have attained that goal.

Repeat this goal brainstorming and prioritisation exercise for each Wheel of Life Dimension you've selected.

Example:

>**Step 1** Wheel of Life dimension: *Physical well-being*
>
>**Step 2** Select the goals that matter. List as many goals as you can think of that would bring about improvement:
>- Lose 15 pounds by eating less
>- Exercise 3-5 times a week
>- Stop drinking sodas
>- Stop snacks between meals
>- No more pastry or ice cream
>- Eat more salads and veggies
>- Cut down on alcohol
>
>**Step 3** Bundle like goals together
>- Lose 15 pounds by eating differently; more salads and veggies and less drinking sodas, snacks, pastry & ice cream, cut down on alcohol
>- Exercise 3-5 times a week
>
>**Step 4** Prioritise goals in order of importance to you
>- Lose 15 pounds by eating differently
>- Exercise 3-5 times a week

Step 5 Rewrite each prioritised goal in positive present-tense language as though it is currently happening.

- 'I maintain my ideal weight by eating nourishing and healthy food and drinks in measured proportions'
- 'I remain fit, flexible and healthy by exercising 3-5 times a week'

Step 6 Once more with feeling...

Step 7 Visualise in your mind's eye what is like to have achieved each goal

SPECIFIC Goal Selection Template

Circle up to 5 dimensions of your Wheel of Life that you feel motivated to take action on:

1. Personal development
2. Work, career, business
3. Relationships, family, children
4. Leisure, sports, hobbies, fun
5. Friends, community involvement, charities
6. Physical well-being, fitness, health, nutrition
7. Spiritual or philosophical interests
8. Finances, savings, debt
9. Physical environment, home
10. Other_____

Wheel of Life Area 1: _____

☐ List goals that would bring about improvement

_____
_____
_____

Step 5: How Are You Getting There?

☐ Bundle Like Goals Together

☐ Prioritise the goals (stick to no more than 3 if you can)

☐ Rewrite each prioritised goal in positive language as though it is currently happening. Be sure to add a 'feeling' word that describes what it feels like to achieve each goal.

☐ Describe (or draw a picture of) what it looks like when you visualise reaching the goal

_____
_____
_____
_____
_____

Repeat the goal-selection process for each Wheel of Life Dimension. Additional Goal-setting worksheets are available at the end of the book.

Goal Achievement Step 2—Measure Success

S	M	A	R	T	E	R
Select Specific Goals	Establish Measures of Success					

'You must have long-range goals to keep you from being frustrated by short-range failures.'

Charles C. Noble

Instructions

The ongoing progress of goal achievement can be measured in at least three timeframes:

1. Short term—today, this week
2. Intermediate term—this month, this quarter
3. Long term—this year, or other increment of years—5, 10, 20, etc.

Milestones

Think of your ultimate long-term milestone in relation to each goal you have selected.

- How will you know when you have successfully achieved each goal?
- When will you achieve it?
- What does it feel like to be in that future space?

Example:

- Goal A—It is (*insert date*) and I easily maintain a healthy weight range of between *x and x* pounds by enjoying measured portions of nutritious food and drink. I am full of energy and feel confident knowing that I look good wearing my favourite outfits.
- Goal B—It is (*insert date*) and I feel fit, flexible, healthy and full of energy and vitality, exercising regularly 3-5 days per week.

Now you try it: Describe your ultimate long-term milestone in relation to each goal you have selected. Record your milestones here, in your journal or in the action planning worksheets at the end of this book.

☐ Wheel of Life Area 1
- Goal A:
- Goal B:
- Goal C:

☐ Wheel of Life Area 2
- Goal A:
- Goal B:
- Goal C:

☐ Wheel of Life Area 3
- Goal A:
- Goal B:
- Goal C:

THE **PERSONAL** ACCOUNTABILITY CODE

- ☐ Wheel of Life Area 4
  - Goal A:
  - Goal B:
  - Goal C:

- ☐ Wheel of Life Area 5
  - Goal A:
  - Goal B:
  - Goal C:

Goal Achievement Step 3—Determine Action Steps

S	M	A	R	T	E	R
Select Specific Goals	Establish Measures of Success	Determine Action Steps				

'The distance between your dreams and reality is called action.'

Unknown

Instructions

Now that you have identified specific goals and what successful goal achievement looks like, what are the action steps or tasks that you will need to work through in order to get there? Action steps can take many forms:

- Doing research
- Accomplishing tasks
- Securing resources (e.g., people, money, time, equipment, tools)
- Closing personal and professional development gaps
- Celebrating milestones

Example:

Action Steps

- ☐ Goal A—It is (*insert date*) and I easily maintain a healthy weight range of between <u>x and x</u> pounds by enjoying measured portions of nutritious food and drink. I am full of energy and feel confident knowing that I look good wearing my favourite outfits.
  - See a doctor about a health and weight check-up by <u>xx</u>
  - See a nutritionist and develop a healthy weight-loss plan by <u>xx</u>
  - Engage accountability partner/join mastermind group… by <u>xx</u> (e.g., coach, peer, Weight Watchers, nutritionist)
  - Establish budget for healthy eating program/Weight Watchers membership
  - Kick off program by <u>xx</u>
  - Establish weekly target weight goals of <u>2 pounds/week</u>
  - Set daily Accountability partnership meetings/phone calls (*dates*)
  - Set celebration milestones (buy that new dress/pair of jeans/splurge on a personal shopping experience)

- ☐ Goal B—It is (*insert date*) and I feel fit, flexible, healthy and full of energy and vitality, exercising regularly 3-5 days per week
  - See a doctor about physical fitness
  - See a personal trainer and develop a fitness schedule
  - Gather resources—budget, training equipment, clothes, memberships, accountability partner
  - Kick off program by <u>xx</u>
  - Establish <u>Weekly Target</u> Fitness goals
  - Set daily Accountability Partnership meetings/phone calls (*dates*)
  - Set celebration milestones

THE **PERSONAL** ACCOUNTABILITY CODE

My Action Steps

In relation to each goal, record the logical action steps you will need to take from where you are now to where you want to be. Record your action steps here, in your journal or in the action planning worksheets at the end of this book.

- ☐ Wheel of Life Area 1
  - Goal A—Action Steps:
  - Goal B—Action Steps:
  - Goal C—Action Steps:

- ☐ Wheel of Life Area 2
  - Goal A—Action Steps:
  - Goal B—Action Steps:
  - Goal C—Action Steps:

- ☐ Wheel of Life Area 3
  - Goal A—Action Steps:
  - Goal B—Action Steps:
  - Goal C—Action Steps:

- ☐ Wheel of Life Area 4
  - Goal A—Action Steps:
  - Goal B—Action Steps:
  - Goal C—Action Steps:

- ☐ Wheel of Life Area 5
  - Goal A—Action Steps
  - Goal B—Action Steps
  - Goal C—Action Steps

Goal Achievement Step 4—Be Realistic

S	M	A	R	T	E	R
Select Specific Goals	Establish Measures of Success	Determine Action Steps	Be Realistic			

'Whenever you're making an important decision, first ask if it gets you closer to your goals or farther way. If the answer is closer, pull the trigger. If it's farther away, make a different choice. Conscious choice making is a critical step in making your dreams a reality.'

Jillian Michaels

Instructions

As with any plan, be it a business plan, financial plan, life plan or career plan, it is important to check in and take stock of whether your goals are realistically aligned with your vision and the resources available to you.

Use the checklist below to review each goal and action step you listed in Step 3. As you are satisfied that each successive goal and action item meets the 'reality check' criteria below, check it off the list. You can enter your checklist results in your journal or the action planning worksheets at the end of this book.

The Reality Checklist

- Does this goal take me closer to my vision for change? If not, make a different choice.
- Am I willing to give up what it takes to achieve my goal e.g. certain foods for a weight loss goal; TV for a fitness or study-related goal
- Are these action steps the best path to my goal?
- Does this goal have enough challenge for me to make it interesting?
- Is this goal too challenging and potentially de-motivating?
- Is this the right time for this goal?

THE PERSONAL ACCOUNTABILITY CODE

- What are the likely obstacles to my achieving this goal or action step?
- Do I have/can I develop the necessary talent and skills?
- Do I have/can I gain access to the required resources?

Goal Achievement Step 5—Align to a Timeframe

S	M	A	R	T	E	R
Select Specific Goals	Establish Measures of Success	Determine Action Steps	Be Realistic	Align to a Timeframe		

'Goals are dreams with deadlines.'

Diana Scarf Hunt

Instructions

In Goal Achievement Step 2 (Milestones), you took the long view as to when you when you would achieve your goals. Now that you have populated and reviewed your action steps, give each of your action items a timeframe. It could be in the form of a specific date (DD/MM/YYY), a timeframe (week, month, 3-6-9-12 months) or a schedule (recurring weekly, fortnightly, monthly).

Example:

☐ Goal A—It is (*insert date*) and I easily maintain a healthy weight range of between *x and x* pounds by enjoying measured portions of nutritious food and drink. I am full of energy and feel confident knowing that I look good wearing my favourite outfits.
  - See a doctor about a health and weight check-up by dd/mm/yyyy
  - Establish Weekly Target Weight goals of *2 pounds/week*

Step 5: How Are You Getting There?

Now return to the action items you listed in Step 3, and insert a date, a timeframe or schedule for each one.

And Now to the Final Instalment of your Personal Accountability Workbook...

By now, you will have created a powerful action plan using the SMART goal-setting method.

My Accountability Action Plan

My Vision & Values Statement :

Wheel of Life Dimension	Specific Goals	Milestones	Action Steps	Reality Check	Time-frame
Health	I easily maintain a healthy weight range	I weigh x lbs by 1st December	Book appointment with doctor Establish weigh in targets Find an accountability partner	y y y	Next week Weekly 2 Weeks

Many goal-setting templates finish here—and this is the problem.

In the next and final instalment of this workbook—Chapter 6—you will add the missing pieces of a winning strategy for goal completion. You will create a SMART+ ER action plan where your natural *Energy* drives forward momentum and a strategy for *Reinforcement* that ensures you stay on track in the face of inevitable obstacles.

Checklist for Chapter 5—How Will I Get There?

- ❏ I have **reviewed my Wheel of Life,** and identified the dimensions where I experience the most dissatisfaction.

- ❏ I have **brainstormed many possible goals within each dimension**, and prioritised the most important to me.

- ❏ I have **written out my goals and action steps using the SMART** goal-setting process.

THE PERSONAL ACCOUNTABILITY CODE™

Step 6: How Will You Stay on Track?

6. NAVIGATION

Purpose of This Chapter

In the previous chapter, you created an action plan for successful goal achievement using the time-tested SMART 5-step goal-setting principles:

Specific—Measurable—Action-oriented—Realistic—Time-Bound

You have now successfully made your way to the final instalment of your *Personal Accountability Code* ™. In this chapter you will add two more steps that will give you the winner's edge by ensuring you remain on track and accountable to your dreams and goals.

The Goal Achievement Steps 6 and 7 take your SMART goals and create an even **SMART + ER** Personal Accountability Action Plan which taps into your personal Energy and Reinforces your progress in the face of obstacles and setbacks.

The SMARTER 7-Step Process for Successful Goal Achievement

- Goal Achievement Step 1—Select **Specific** Goals (Chapter 5)
- Goal Achievement Step 2—Establish **Measures** of Success (Chapter 5)
- Goal Achievement Step 3—Determine **Action** Steps (Chapter 5)
- Goal Achievement Step 4—Be **Realistic** (Chapter 5)
- Goal Achievement Step 5—Align to a **Timeframe** (Chapter 5)
- Goal Achievement Step 6—Ensure goals are **Energising** (Chapter 6)
- Goal Achievement Step 7—**Reinforce** progress (Chapter 6)

Goal Achievement Step 6—Energised: You will leverage your existing strengths by tapping into natural sources of positive energy and drive that are unique to you; and

Goal Achievement Step 7—Reinforced: You will mitigate the threat of giving up by installing a powerful system of positive reinforcement to keep you on track, including positive supportive review through feedback; feedforward and follow-through to carry you through the inevitable obstacles ahead; and personalised rewards to recognise and celebrate your progress.

Step 6: How Will You Stay on Track?

With these final two steps, 6 and 7, in play, you will have the ultimate Personal Accountability Action Plan, together with an accountability tracking system you are unlikely to wriggle out of as soon as something goes wrong—which it will!

And what an amazing opportunity life presents us if things *do* go wrong: in this chapter, we see how setbacks, obstacles and failures can be amongst our most valuable defining moments, both personally and professionally—moments that can propel us into the stratosphere of personal growth and achievement.

Exercises:

The SMARTER 7-Step Process for Successful Goal Achievement

- Goal Achievement Step 6—Ensure goals are **Energising**
- Goal Achievement Step 7—**Reinforce** progress

Goal Achievement Step 6—Ensure Goals are Energising

S	M	A	R	T	E	R
Select Specific Goals	Establish Measures of Success	Determine Action Steps	Be Realistic	Align to a Timeframe	Ensure Goals are Energising	

'Follow your passion. Stay true to yourself. Never follow someone else's path unless you're in the woods and you're lost and you see a path. By all means, you should follow that.'

Ellen DeGeneres

Instructions:

Review your personal analysis and reflections from Chapter 3 *'Who Are You?'* and Chapter 4 *'SPOT Analysis'*.

Optimise your environment for goal-achieving success by using the following checklist to ensure your goals and action items are personally energising, motivating and inspiring:

- ☐ My goals are consistent with my principal **drives and motivations**
- ☐ My goals leverage m**y strengths**
- ☐ Where some goals require skills or experience I don't possess to the level required, I am closing this **skill/experience gap** either by
  - adding a specific personal or professional development goal
  - acquiring a resource to cover off where I don't excel

Now use these insights about your unique sources of energy and motivation, to create additional goals or action items.

Goal Achievement Step 7—Reinforce Progress

S	M	A	R	T	E	R
Select Specific Goals	Establish Measures of Success	Determine Action Steps	Be Realistic	Align to a Timeframe	Ensure Goals are Energising	Reinforce Progress

'You are more likely to hold yourself accountable for goals that others know about. Tell someone what you're up to.'

Unknown

How to Handle Setbacks, Obstacles and Failure

Memorable setbacks, obstacles and failures can be amongst our most valuable and defining moments both personally and professionally. Depending on how we handle them, they can potentially be moments that propel us into the stratosphere of personal growth and achievement or regrets that bring back bad memories of resentment, pain and blame.

See if you can think back on two scenarios from your past experience. The first scenario: Briefly think of a time when your intentions were thwarted by a setback, obstacle or failure. Your memory of that time probably brings back difficult memories of pain and resentment. You might even be able to picture someone or something you can apportion blame to. Just think of it for a moment—don't write it down or dwell on it here. I don't want you to reinforce the memory.

Now turn your attention to another time when things didn't go to plan—yet you made it through and recall it with fonder memories. Describe what happened:

_____

_____

On reflection, why do you recall this as a more positive experience than your earlier example?

_____

_____

The **Personal** Accountability Code™

It is often the case that our experience of setback, obstacles and failure depends on a couple of things:

- the degree to which we take accountability for our role in the outcome and/or
- ownership for our response to the situation, no matter how dire.

Only when we approach setback from these perspectives (either on our own or with a little help from a coach) can we break through and see alternative pathways to personal growth, development and success. If we remain mired in apportioning blame elsewhere, we give away our power and become a victim of circumstance.

> *'Experience is not what happens to a man; it is what a man does with what happens to him.'*
>
> **Aldous Huxley**

In a study of 200 prominent public and private sector leaders, authors Warren Bennis and Robert Thomas found that each leader could almost always point to an intensely traumatic and often unplanned experience in their career that led to their most defining moments of personal and professional growth (*Crucibles of Leadership*, 2008, Harvard Business Review Press). They accepted accountability for their role in the situation, learned from their mistakes and honed their skills—becoming better people, better professionals because of it.

Regardless of whether you carry the official title of leader or not, these findings apply to you. You don't need to carry the official title of 'leader' to be a leader. If you have been working your way through *The Personal Accountability Code*™, you are clearly taking the leadership reins of your life to unlock your greatest potential for personal fulfilment, success and achievement.

It can be difficult to view a setback with objectivity when you are in the middle of it. These are the times when a coach becomes an invaluable partner in helping you reframe obstacles as goals through the lens of opportunity.

The Reality of Personal Transformation

'Success is the progressive realisation of a worthy goal or ideal.'
Earl Nightingale

The reality of personal transformation is that it is a process rather than a destination. Staying accountable to your goals requires a system—not just a heading and an action plan. Many a goal seeker has fallen off the rails, deflated when things didn't go to plan, or disappointed that they had not 'transformed' according to a predetermined schedule.

The magic of personal transformation is much bigger than a defined event in time and takes place:

- In the new habits you cultivate as a result of deciding to do some small thing every day to achieve your goals
- Through the wisdom you acquire when things don't go to plan and you need to correct or change your course of action
- Inside of the strength, character and personal resilience you develop along the way, which buoys you through obstacles and setbacks
- When those around you progressively start to see that you have changed

In fact, to focus obsessively on the destination can cruelly rob you of the lasting benefits of genuine personal transformation. An inflexible attachment to the end goal may blind you to the signs that you need to correct course. An overriding focus on the destination as the only hallmark of success saps your energy and is difficult to sustain over the medium to long term. Failure to stop to renew your energy and appreciate your progress can lead to chronic feelings of failure, disappointment and frustration.

For some who achieve their goals through extreme (although temporary) willpower, perhaps the ultimate irony is that, by failing to appreciate the process of personal transformation, achieving the end game may quickly turn sour. After all, once you achieve your ultimate goal under these circumstances—what else is there after the goal is reached? Some of the greatest achievers in the sports arena have succumbed to despair and depression because they weren't prepared for what comes after the accolades have faded. For a handy checklist of issues like this to watch out for when it comes to derailing from our goals, refer to Appendix 1—*The Do's and Don'ts of Personal Accountability*.

Systems for Keeping Track of Personal Goals

As the real benefits of personal transformation occur in the progressive actions we take every day to do something differently, a guide to personal goal achievement would be incomplete without an overview of the types of ways you can track your goals.

Accountability Partnerships: Nothing comes close to the power of accountability partnerships when it comes to keeping you on track towards your goals, especially when things get tough or you want (or need) a different perspective. Whether this is achieved through a professional coaching arrangement or a peer relationship, the act of sharing your progress with another human being who cares enough to hold you to account is a phenomenal motivator.

In this guide, you won't find me recommending a specific system for tracking your goals beyond the principles of accountability partnerships. This is because the accountability code is about decoding a winning strategy that works for *you*, to transform your goals and dreams from strategy through to reality. I can't tell you which goal-tracking system is right for you—only you can work that out, but the following is a range of tracking systems you can try out:

Manual Goal-Tracking Systems: Starting with your Accountability Action Plan, you can keep track of daily, weekly and monthly progress with something as simple as a diary or a spreadsheet. A journal is another good idea to keep track of your thoughts and insights.

Online Goal-Tracking Systems: If you want to get more sophisticated, you can try out the online environment with various project management, time management and goal-tracking programs and apps based on your personality, preferences and lifestyle. There are a bunch of free and paid services. Some examples of high rating goal—tracking apps and software are: **Strides—Goals & Habits Tracker; Full; Way of Life—The Ultimate Habit Maker & Breaker; Joe's Goals; 43 Things; Lifetick; GoalsOnTrack;** and **Goalscape.** You can even find apps for specific goals such as **Calorie Counter & Diet Tracker** and **RunKeeper—GPS Running, Walk, Cycling, Cardio and Weight Tracking**.

Step 6: How Will You Stay on Track?

Mastermind Groups: Mastermind groups are another way to drive progress, through getting together with others who share similar personal or professional development objectives.

Instructions:

Drive home your goal-achieving success by selecting your own personal system of positive reinforcement, review and reward to keep you on track and support you in the face of inevitable obstacles. Refer to your insights from your strengths, problems and habits analysis in Chapter 4, Chapter 1 (Are You Ready for Change) and Chapter 3 (What Drives You: Compelling Consequences) and *'How I handle setbacks'* in Chapter 6.

Now use the following personal accountability checklist to add the final goals and action items to your Personal Accountability Action Plan.

- ❐ I have reviewed my **Personal Accountability and Responsibility development objectives** and included those in my action plan as personal development goals (Chapter 1).
- ❐ I have reflected on how I handled **setbacks** in the past and am prepared to approach a coach or accountability partner to help me through when inevitable setbacks occur in the future (Chapter 6).
- ❐ I have reviewed the **habits** that either undermine or reinforce my goals and intentions. If required, to achieve my goals, I have added a new habit that I want to acquire into my personal development objectives (Chapter 4).
- ❐ I have included a specific goal and action items for entering into an **accountability partnership or coaching engagement** as part of my action plan (Chapter 1).
- ❐ I have recorded a (potential) **schedule of feedback** with my accountability partner or coach on how and how often we will touch base (Chapter 1).
- ❐ I have reviewed how to **ask others for feedback** so I can learn more about myself and track my progress (Chapter 1).
- ❐ I have identified the compelling consequences that work as rewards to **celebrate the small wins** as I progress towards my goals. I have added celebratory milestones to my action plan at key points (Chapter 3).
- ❐ I have identified a **goal-tracking system** that works for me (Chapter 6).

Winning with Personal Accountability & Goals

Congratulations on completing *The Personal Accountability Code*™!

You are now in possession of one of the most powerful personalised goal-achievement toolkits available.

I believe that the missing piece in most goal-setting programs is the new science of accountability. Lack of accountability—to oneself, to each other—is the #1 goal buster of all time.

There are plenty of common traps we fall into when we set goals. I have included a list of the most common goal busters and how to deal with them in **Appendix 1: *Do's and Don'ts of Winning with Personal Accountability.***

When we say we take responsibility for our health, our work, our relationships, and set goals, and then end up doing the same things, we're fooling ourselves. That's a trap you don't want to perpetuate.

But with a system of accountability and an accountability partner—or a coach—or someone else involved in our goals, we are more likely to make progress.

It's too easy to move the goal posts when you're the only one on the field. Marshall Goldsmith, an expert in bringing about behavioural change in leaders, says in his book *What Got You Here Won't Get You There* that without follow-up, people don't get better. With follow-up, they do.

It's that simple.

It will hurt.
It will take time.
It will require dedication.
It will require willpower.
You will need to make healthy decisions.
It requires sacrifice.
There will be temptation.
But, I promise you, when you reach your goal,
It's WORTH it.

Unknown

To Your Goal-Achieving Success!

DI WORRALL

THE **PERSONAL** ACCOUNTABILITY CODE

Checklist for Chapter 6—How Will I Stay on Track?

☐ I have reviewed my action plan to ensure it aligns with my greatest sources of **energy** and drive using the SMARTER goal-setting system

☐ I will ensure that my action plan has a built-in **reinforcement** system of personal accountability that will help me overcome obstacles and keep me on track towards my goals

☐ I have selected a **goal-tracking system** that works for me

THE PERSONAL ACCOUNTABILITY CODE™

The Accountability Coach

Solving 6 Common Dilemmas about Goal Achievement and Personal Accountability

The **Personal** Accountability Code

1. Getting Back on Track After a Setback

Let's face it—willpower fails all of us at some point.

How many people have started their new year's resolutions with the best of intentions, only to reach February and look back in disgust that they didn't follow through? We are masters of excuses. Here are some of the more common ones that derail our plans:

- A great idea didn't get off the drawing board
- Lacked focus and direction so unclear how to start
- Life got in the way
- Your job got in the way
- Fear of what could go wrong stopped you from taking action
- Lost motivation, inspiration or sense of urgency
- Got frustrated and gave up
- Too many other stressors
- An external event, circumstance, resource or person got in the way or let you down
- Not enough time or resources
- Wrong skill set
- Too many to dos, so you don't
- You started but failed to stay on task, and gave up too quickly

You can choose to dwell on yet another failure and allow it to define you, or you can choose to move beyond it.

There are two ways to deal with setback:

1. Plan for the likelihood that failure and setback *will* occur; and
2. Get back on track

Plan for Failure in Advance

In the *Personal Accountability Code*™ you are encouraged to get clear on the things that are likely to cause you to slip up, and plan for them in advance. You also look at the things that are your greatest sources of strength and motivation. That way, when setback does occur, it will be less of a shock, and you will be able to use your strengths as an anchor and your risk management plans to bounce back much faster.

Plan for setback with the following activities:

1. Confront your readiness for responsibility and accountability and take steps to address any issues where you tend to fall short
2. Engage a coach, friend or colleague who can be your accountability partner
3. Understand where your deepest priorities come from by getting your values and goals in sync
4. Know the source of your energy and vitality—your strengths, what really drives you and motivates you to action. Build your plans around these where possible. Conversely, knowing what you are *not* good at and what *demotivates* you allows you to plan around this as well, by either eliminating or mitigating these factors where you can
5. Consider the resources and opportunities available to you, as well as the resources you don't have and the potential threats to your plans which may lie outside of your direct control
6. Be really specific about your goal/s in the first place, doing your best to record and quantify each of the action steps it will take to get there and planning for what might go wrong along the way
7. Be realistic about your goals, expecting that some of the details around the time-frame and pathway to get there may change along the way if other circumstances and priorities arise
8. Have your follow-up system in place before you rush headlong into your goal-achievement activities

6 Steps to Get Back on Track

Having taken steps to soften the blow of setback, the reality of any worthwhile goal is that setback and failure will still happen. Here are 6 tips to get back on track after a setback. *(See Attachment 1.0 for a handy checklist of solutions to common derailers of goal-achieving success: The Dos and Don'ts of personal accountability.)*

1. Don't beat yourself up or blame others
2. Seek out the support of an accountability partner
3. Accept setback, learn from it, be grateful for the learning—and let it go
4. Realise that tomorrow is a new day with a fresh, clean slate
5. Remind yourself what you HAVE done to make progress towards your goal
6. Set aside some time in your diary intentionally to do something (anything), no matter how small, which is related to your goal.

If you are feeling the frustration of a major setback, try the following stress-reducing activity:

Find a quiet place alone, or with your accountability partner, and answer the following questions:

- What has gone well in the achievement of your goal?
- Acknowledge the progress you made.
- What hasn't gone as well as you would have liked?
- If something hasn't gone so well, could you do anything about it?
- If so, what are you going to do about it and when?
- If not, choose to let it go

2. How to Hold Others Accountable

Because we don't live in a vacuum, at one time or another you will need to gain someone else's co-operation in order to achieve your personal, professional, team or corporate goals.

Unfortunately, when it comes to our greatest fears, if public speaking is #1, then the thought of confronting an issue of poor accountability with someone would be in the vicinity of #2. Hence our lack of practice means that our skills tend to be poor to average at best in holding high accountability conversations when times are tough. This certainly holds true in my experience as an executive coach. I have found that even the most seasoned chief executive can benefit from a little coaching in holding others accountable for the delivery of results.

Why exactly is the prospect of holding others accountable so distasteful? We have an emotional argument that tells us that conversations that are challenging and potentially confronting are uncomfortable. Why volunteer for an uncomfortable conversation if we don't have to? Especially if it risks meaning we won't be liked, or degenerates into undesirable consequences like a verbal backlash, rejection, or looking foolish. Let's face it; for some who are not in a position of power, standing up to someone who *is* could be a career-limiting move.

Holding People Accountable—Guidelines for Leaders

The Consequences for Leaders Who Fail to Hold Teams Accountable

For leaders in particular, we can create a smorgasbord of plausible logical arguments in support of our decision to turn a blind eye to failures in accountability:

- There is not enough time to set aside to develop accountability in others because we are under-resourced, overworked and overloaded
- It's easier to find a good excuse to move someone out of the team or onto a special project
- I'll just put up with the issue and ignore it—these things usually work themselves out

- My staff either can't handle it or don't want to step up to accountability
- I have too many other priorities for me to waste time developing improved accountability in others who aren't up to it
- I get by doing the work myself or by relying on a small circle of people whom I know and can trust to deliver
- It's better not to cause upset and rock the boat by rewarding some and not others, even if they are under-performing
- I work best under pressure and in a crisis. After all, that's what it is like around here
- As far as I am aware, I made my expectations very clear; I don't understand why they don't follow through on what they've been instructed to do
- I can put up with one of my star performers' problems with some aspects of poor accountability because I am concerned they will leave if I confront them

While these excuses would be familiar to leaders, many are equally applicable to those who need to rely on other people to achieve goals.

It might seem easier to put up with failures in accountability in the short term rather than confront the issue head on. However, this approach is not without consequence. Failure to interrupt this pattern means that you, your team, and anyone else who is part of your goal-achievement network will continue to experience the negative consequences of poor accountability such as work overload, frustration and crisis due to poor accountability. By assigning reliable employees extra work, you are perceived to be rewarding under-performers with a lighter workload. If you do not acknowledge the different levels of contribution, employees can feel demoralised and the performance of the whole team suffers. As a leader, you run the very real risk of others perceiving you as someone who: is a weak leader incapable of leading or managing others; is a poor delegator; withholds opportunities; and hogs the limelight. Poor skills in holding others accountable can lead to you being perceived as unfair, either playing favourites with some or condoning unacceptable behaviour and under-performance from others, allowing them to freeload without consequence.

The ultimate price you pay for this perception is your standing as a leader and the respect and trust people have in you to make decisions and set the tone and direction. It's the job of the leader to step up, set the standards and make the time. If *you* don't stop the excuses, blame and denial, who else is going to do it? The buck needs to stop somewhere.

The reality of this dilemma is that it is far more difficult to regain trust and respect once it is compromised than it is to invest your best efforts in creating a high-accountability culture in the first place.

A Checklist for Leaders for Holding Team Members Accountable
While we often use the phrase 'holding others accountable' in relation to a leader's job, it is far more productive to focus more of our attention on creating the conditions for a high-accountability culture to grow, develop and thrive. When you create the conditions for accountability, team members are more likely to hold themselves accountable, and leaders will rarely be required to step in and 'hold' people accountable. Holding people to account would only occur following unmet expectations and failed agreements. The following checklist aids in creating the conditions for high team accountability:

Model accountability. If you want team members to change their behaviour, demonstrate it yourself first. Understand the strength of your responsibility and accountability muscles and be a model of high accountability. Close any gaps with some good coaching.

Clarify expectations of what high accountability looks like. Holding a workshop to define high accountability is a highly worthwhile team development exercise enabling a team and the team leader to address historical issues and look to the future by establishing the new rules of accountability for how they fulfil commitments to themselves as individuals, to each other, to the leader (and vice versa) as well as to the organisation, clients and other stakeholders.

Define roles and responsibilities. Lines of accountability and responsibility are blurring in today's fast-paced, complex and global business landscape. By establishing this clarity you take the vital first steps to developing an agreed benchmark against which you can hold someone accountable. Clarifying expectations applies not only to leaders and their subordinate teams, but also to colleagues, peers and service providers who are working with you to achieve goals.

Clarify handover points and escalation points. In modern complex organisations, perceptions of organisational hierarchy are changing. Structures are getting flatter and jobs are designed to be more interdependent than ever. While these are great intentions, more flexible job designs mean that there is vastly more opportunity for responsibility and accountability to fall between the cracks when one task is handed over to another position to fulfil. It is vitally important for position holders to regularly interact with their colleagues and team leaders to define handover points and escalation points.

Seek commitment, alignment and share the urgency. Don't expect accountability to be forthcoming in others as a consequence of your position. The world has changed and you need to invite people to engage with and connect with your goals and objectives on a personal level. Using the WIFM rule ('What's in it for me?') to demonstrate what success looks like, explain the urgency and how your goals *will* benefit those you are working with—your team, peers, colleagues or the organisation.

Agree on consequences. What happens when agreed expectations are: 1) met and 2) unmet? We typically associate consequences with punitive and short term rewards and punishments. While this approach yields some success impacting short term behaviour, the more effective and compelling consequences target how people *feel* about work. This has far greater impact motivating performance and higher accountability in the longer term. Map out your team's compelling consequences by first asking what motivates and incentivises them to do something new or different e.g. pay and privileges. Then complete the picture by finding out how they would like to experience work e.g. recognition, inclusion, acknowledgement, visibility. Taking positive consequences away when expectations are unmet, creates negative consequences. For further information on compelling consequences, see *Accountability Leadership* 2013, D Worrall.

Establish clear agreements. Lock down commitments with voluntary written and signed agreements. Clear agreements are an important benchmark for accountability, describing specific goals, who does what, to what standard of measurement and by when. Sharing agreements with those who will be impacted by them is an added incentive to stay committed and accountable.

Provide Support and Resources. It's impossible to be accountable if you don't have sufficient resources, training, accountability, authority or support to deliver on your agreements. As a leader, set your team up for success by supplying these resources and conveying your confidence in their ability to deliver.

Inspire and Motivate. Leaders have an enormous capacity to inspire high accountability by influencing people's emotions and how they *feel* about work. However, it is important to find out exactly what motivates employees instead of making blind assumptions. This was borne out in a study by Amabile and Kramer, where managers ranked 'recognition' and 'incentives' as the most important factors in motivating people, with 'progress' dead last. Interestingly, employees ranked 'progress' as the most important factor resulting from a leader's ability to acknowledge the small wins.

Determine how follow-up will be handled. Most leaders understand that consistent follow-up is a key component of accountability and evaluating performance. However, this can be easier said than done. Determine which form follow-up will take, who will do it (leaders, teams, peers) and how often. Good follow-up is frequent and includes both feedback on past performance and feedforward on suggestions for future improvement. Courageous leaders understand that the best follow-up for high-accountability cultures functions in multiple dimensions: from leader to employee; from employee to leader; and peer to peer.

Finally, hold yourself accountable for creating the conditions for high accountability. If you need help growing your skills in this area, invite your accountability partner or coach to lend a hand.

> *For a comprehensive guidebook on leadership accountability, pick up a copy of the Amazon bestseller 'Accountability Leadership' (2013) Di Worrall.*

Holding People Accountable—Guidelines for Individuals and Teams

The Consequences of Failing to Hold Your Peers Accountable

Sometimes we need to get things done through other people when we are not in a position of power. You might be a project or change manager, team member, colleague or customer. You could be seeking to influence others in your team, in other teams or across disparate locations locally or abroad.

The most obvious risk of failing to hold others accountable is that goals might not be fulfilled. The less obvious risk is that such failures are likely to reflect straight back at you.

By far the most popular excuse in failures of this kind is that you didn't have the power or authority to hold others accountable. While this may be true at times, it is more frequently the case that you didn't step up into your own personal power using influence and persuasion. Your personal power to influence and persuade can have a far more lasting impact on someone's behaviour and attitude than the power of position. Issuing commands by way of positional power can have an immediate impact on short-term activities, but is notoriously ineffective in creating the conditions for high accountability through engagement, loyalty, trust and discretionary effort over the longer term.

In addition to the convenient excuse of not having positional authority, there are many other excuses that get in the way of holding peers accountable to their promises:

- There is not enough time to follow up people who don't pull their weight because I am under-resourced, overworked and overloaded
- It's easier to just get someone else to deliver—someone I trust, such as a co-worker, team member, supplier
- I'll just put up with the issue and ignore it—these things usually work themselves out
- The people around me either can't handle it or don't want to step up to accountability
- I have too many other priorities for me to waste time developing improved accountability in others who aren't up to it
- I get better results doing the work myself

- It's best not to call out unaccountable behaviour because I don't want to appear as pushy and demanding and risk upsetting someone
- Calling out unaccountable behaviour is not in my job description
- I work best under pressure and in a crisis
- As far as I am aware, I made my expectations very clear; I don't understand why they don't follow through on what they've been asked to do
- I can put up with a key person's poor accountability because I am concerned they won't continue to support me if I confront their behaviour

What is particularly interesting about this list is that these excuses are nearly identical to the excuses that leaders give for not holding staff accountable.

The Lesson: Positional power is not an automatic fix for unaccountable behaviour in yourself or others.

For each of these excuses that we use to justify our not holding our peers accountable, there are negative consequences which are not as obvious as failing to achieve your goals:

- You, your colleagues, and anyone else who is part of your goal-achievement network will experience the negative consequences of poor accountability such as work overload, frustration and crises
- By failing to hold your peers to account, you unwittingly contribute to undermining the morale of you and your fellow team memberswho may feel demoralised and resentful of "freeloaders" who demonstrate consistently unaccountable behaviour without consequence.

Even without positional authority, being someone who stands for something, gets things done, follows up and does what they say earns you trust and respect. If you don't stand up for something, you risk falling for anything, being taken advantage of and exploited. *You* ultimately set the tone for how you are treated by other people. If you don't stop the excuses, blame and denial, who else is going to do it? The buck needs to stop somewhere.

The reality of this dilemma is that it is far more difficult to regain trust and respect once it is compromised than it is to invest your best efforts in creating the conditions for high accountability around you in the first place.

A Checklist for Holding Others Accountable When You Don't Have the Authority
How do you influence people to commit to and deliver on outcomes when you don't have the authority?

We have seen that positional power is not an automatic fix for dealing with unaccountable behaviour in yourself and other people. This doesn't mean you have to become a member of the 'accountability police'. You have many options available to exercise your personal power and influence to encourage high accountability in others you don't have authority over. The following are some suggestions for encouraging high accountability at work:

> *To influence without positional power, use your circle of influence: other team members, peers and direct supervisors*

Work on your own accountability 'ability'. Prepare yourself for stepping up to accountability. Take the responsibility- and accountability-readiness assessment. If you need a little coaching, go and get it.

Create a team accountability code. Say you are part of a group of people who are assigned the achievement of a particular goal. Consider this group of people a team. Whether the team is a formal part of an organisational structure or a more loosely structured and informal team, the team environment nonetheless is part of your circle of influence. When harnessed, teams can carry a powerful motivating force of accountability to drive results, due to the peer pressure. Place accountability on the team agenda and brainstorm, together with the other team members, suggestions for a mutual 'team accountability code' of conduct.

Work with team members' supervisors to clarify and endorse their roles, responsibilities and priorities inside of your project or task.

Clarify all agreements, goals and measures in writing with everyone involved and publicise (voluntarily) these agreements with team members.

Share the responsibility for follow-up within the team rather than just you personally handling it.

Brainstorm the nature of consequences with the team including what reward and recognition looks like and the consequences of unmet expectations.

Encourage a sense of commitment and urgency by helping your peers to understand the context of the goal—what's in it for them, the impact of their commitment on other team members, on stakeholders and the broader organisation.

Model accountability by following through on your own promises and commitments.

3. How to Deal with Unmet Expectations, Broken Promises and Failed Commitments

Even with the best of intentions, at times we all fail to meet expectations, break promises and renege on commitments.

These bumps in accountability can look like:

- Missed deadlines
- Disruptions
- Being late
- Not pulling your weight
- Failing to do what you said you would do in whole or in part
- Forgetting
- Sidestepping your failures with blame, excuses and denial

In the event that expectations are unmet, there is a right and wrong way to deal with these types of failures in accountability.

What to do if you break an agreement—the wrong way
- Ignore your mishap
- Fail to acknowledge the impact you have had on someone else
- Offer your best excuses, blame or denial routine

What to do if you break an agreement—the right way
Realise that your action or inaction may have caused upset, aggravation and annoyance. Your credibility may be compromised and trust in you bruised.

Take steps to redeem the situation and your relationship with the people you affected:

- Acknowledge the situation and its impact
- Accept responsibility and apologise
- Ask about the impact on the person/people you affected and listen—don't argue or respond defensively
- Renegotiate what you agreed to do and by when
- Resolve to deliver on your promise

If in the future if you anticipate that you aren't going to meet expectations, it is always advisable to let those you made the promise to know beforehand.

If this seems like a pattern or habit for you—e.g., always turning up late to meetings—engage your coach or a friend, family member or work colleague as an accountability partner to help you out with:

1. Feedforward suggestions as to how you can become an 'on-time' person; and
2. Holding you accountable for putting your new behaviour in place until it becomes more habitual

What to do if someone else breaks an agreement—the wrong way
- Ignore it or complain behind their back
- Demonstrate frustration and anger
- Threaten with an undesirable consequence
- Launch into a tirade of blame and accusation
- Overload the conversation with a raft of 'you' statements
- Take control and micromanage

What to do if someone else breaks an agreement—the right way
- Find neutral territory where you can call out the broken agreement
- Take a calming breath
- Refer to the specific agreement or promise that has been violated and enquire as to what happened
- Use 'I' statements to clarify the impact on you or the team. A good rule of thumb is to express yourself with regard to how it is for you and not how the other person 'should' have behaved; e.g., 'I noticed that... tell me about it'
- Invite a renegotiation to plan out how the broken agreement will be addressed
- Clarify the consequences of failing to deliver again
- If you are a leader, ensure your employee has adequate resources, skills, authority and tools to fulfil the agreement
- Allow them the opportunity to deliver on the new terms; resist the urge to control and micromanage

If expectations are once again unmet, enquire as to why. Be wary of repeat excuses—else you will be taken advantage of. It is important that you follow through on the consequences you agreed if there are no reasonable extenuating circumstances.

4. How to be Motivated When Goals Have Been Imposed Upon You

While it's true that pursuing your own personal vision and goals can ignite a powerful drive and motivation to succeed, it does not follow that pursuing someone *else's* goals and expectations has to be *demotivating*.

The trick to uncovering the source of your energy and motivation in these circumstances is to take a moment to connect the dots between the 'imposed' goals and your higher goals and intentions.

Finding your motivation—Scenario 1: Let's start with a big-picture scenario to illustrate the point. We don't live in isolation. We pursue our own goals within the context of a much broader community which sets certain expectations in exchange for the right to co-exist and be accepted by others. We are either consciously or unconsciously motivated to adhere to those expectations in order to:

- Embrace a primal need to exist—and, ideally, prosper—within that community; and
- Avoid the potentially unpleasant consequences of either being ostracised from or penalised by that community

For example, various laws are imposed upon us that set down the rules governing society. You might not agree with some of those laws. However, the vast majority of people are motivated to abide by laws they don't necessary like (or break laws in such a way that they hope not to get caught) in order to maintain a place in their community and avoid any unpleasant consequences of being penalised or rejected.

How about the work environment?

Assuming your boss is reasonable and competent; you are asked you to pursue a goal which in itself appears of no direct benefit or interest to you. Pause for a moment to connect the dots from their goals to your own and see where they meet up. Some examples are listed hereunder.

Finding your motivation—Scenario 2: You are asked to prepare a report for a boss that doesn't interest you and necessitates you rearranging other work in order to complete it. You could respond in several ways:

- Accept the assignment without question but begrudgingly make an effort to rearrange your schedule to complete the report. You demonstrate your dissatisfaction passively aggressively through procrastination or by preparing the report half-heartedly. The risk with these approaches is that the report is complete but not on time or up to an appropriate standard. Submitting poor-quality work late will not reflect well on perceptions of your capacity, interest or career potential.

    This approach turns out not to be consistent with your real motivation of career progression.

- Accept the assignment, rearrange your schedule and hold yourself accountable to your promise by preparing the report on time and to the best of your ability. By doing so, you do your boss a favour and get her out of a bind. Not only that; she thinks better of you, perceives you as loyal, easy to work with and someone who gets things done. You are perceived as someone who knows how to prioritise the organisation's interests over their own, and as such are likely to be considered favourably when even bigger opportunities come around in the future. You are developing a productive relationship with someone who may even be an advocate for your career advancement.

    This approach is consistent with your real motivation of career progression, rewards and positive recognition.

Finding your motivation—some more scenarios:

- You are asked by the human resources department to attend a professional-development class in leadership soft skills, which you are not interested in and are too busy to attend. You decide to pursue the class anyway and give it your fullest attention. In the process, you learn something new and have a broader skill base to draw upon at work. Your new skill is noticed by the people around you and by your boss. You are perceived as more effective and others perceive you as willing and able to pursue greater opportunities.

This new learning is a stepping stone to what you are really motivated by—a promotion into leadership.

- You are approached by a project manager to co-ordinate a particular aspect of an organisational project. This work will significantly increase your workload for a period of time as it will be on top of business-as-usual activities and there is no extra remuneration involved. You accept the assignment and rearrange your schedule accordingly. You learn many new things. You gain hands-on experience of co-ordinating others across functions and during periods of significant change as well as of more efficient ways for getting the work done. You make mistakes but also get to learn from them and correct them—an opportunity you can't find in a textbook. You find a sense of satisfaction tackling something that others shy away from. The way others see you forever changes. You become an inspiration and role model for others, who see you as having the courage to step up to the challenge and succeed.

  This new project opportunity is consistent with what you are really motivated by— inspiring people to step up to a challenge, standing out from your peers and being seen as having greater potential and influence beyond your regular team.

- You are asked by a friend or community group to offer your time and effort to help towards the achievement of their goal. You willingly volunteer your time.

  To simply be of service is a powerful motivator in its own right, in the knowledge that you have helped someone or something out when they needed a hand.

We live in connectivity with other people. Connecting someone else's goals to your own is a really valuable skill to master, both for your own satisfaction and goal achievement, and for the enhancement of the community around you. You will also be in a much better position to inspire others in the future when the tables are turned and it is your turn to get people on board with your goals.

5. 10 of the Best Tips for Overcoming Procrastination

Are you being honest with yourself about the cause of your procrastination? Brendon Burchard, author of *Life's Golden Ticket (2009)* and *The Motivation Manifesto* (2014), challenges procrastinators to think hard about regurgitating *perfectionism* as your excuse for failing to move an important task forward. He warns that perfectionism is in reality a 'sexy' cover-up for the deeper problems of allowing yourself to get distracted from your priorities through poor habits of personal organisation, fear and self-doubt.

The truth can be quite confronting.

What signs of procrastination are you leaving in your wake? Are you spending excessive time on a task, endlessly 'adding value' to it? Are you acting out your favourite avoidance behaviours like eating outside of normal mealtimes, suddenly feeling too tired to continue, cleaning the house (again), surfing the Net, chatting on social media, checking your emails, watching TV, leaving things until the last minute, putting it off until you're in the right frame of mind or it is the right time? Procrastination could also be your mind and body telling that you are experiencing serious stress overload somewhere in your life.

First the bad news: Chronic procrastination can be a sign of much deeper fears, anxieties and stress. It is important that you take steps to address your underlying psychological health, which is beyond the scope of this book. *If this is the case for you, reach out to a trusted friend or medical/psychology professional.*

Further, according to psychologists, some people are fundamentally procrastinator-type personalities. Certain personality tests administered by accredited individuals can be an indicator of this type, as can your own experience of a compulsive *addiction* to avoidance of tasks. This experience of procrastination is far more pervasive—more like a stubborn habit or *soft* addiction. This procrastinator has very low impulse control and self-discipline and is easily distracted. The solutions offered in the following list are likely to be ineffective in isolation—as the moderator of the online community *Procrastinators Anonymous* points out:

> *'If you give a procrastinator a new time management tool, he will just play with the new time management tool as a way to procrastinate. The problem is not a*

lack of time management skills—or not mainly a lack of time management skills. Procrastination is a form of addictive escapism that must be dealt with directly or there will be no recovery.'

If you are concerned that procrastination is undermining your quality of life in this regard, it is again recommended that you contact a medical/psychology professional or reach out to a support group such as the online community *Procrastinators Anonymous*.

For those of you who only put certain things off from time to time, try some of the following 10 suggestions for beating procrastination.

1. **Tackle something small and easy first.** The thought of everything required to achieve a big goal can be overwhelming. Try tackling something small first so you can enjoy the sense of accomplishment and satisfaction that comes with completion.

2. **If 'easy' has you stumped, then take action on *anything* productive**—so long as you do it now. Overthinking—like over-planning—can also lead nowhere. If you can't find a place to start, try the two-minute rule from Dave Allen's book, *Getting Things Done*: 'If it takes less than two minutes, *DO IT NOW*.' Any progress on *something* is a lot better than a whole lot of *nothing*.

3. **Find your distraction-free environment.** Organise your environment to be free of distraction and conducive to working on an important goal. That might involve being comfortable and quiet, having all your tools around you, and drinks and snacks within easy access. Turn off distractions like mobile devices and ask people to either be quiet or stay away while you are working. When I find the distractions of my usual working environment taking over at the expense of an important writing or editing deadline, I head to a local coffee shop where there is no other option except to focus on the task at hand. In exchange for a table and a cup of coffee, I can achieve a laser-like sense of focus and urgency to drive several hours of highly productive concentration when I need it most. An overwhelming sense of accomplishment is my reward, which then spills over into a renewed focus when I return to my workplace.

4. **Focus and prioritise.** When you have too many to dos—you don't. Working through the 6 steps of *The Personal Accountability Code*™ provides a structure and system of accountability that will enable you to focus only on your highest priorities and goals in each area of your life.

5. **Break it down.** A familiar procrastination story is the rush and urgency to complete something that has been left to the last minute. However, breaking down larger tasks into smaller chunks over a longer period offers more benefits than alleviating undue pressure and stress on you and those around you that it affects. Breaking down larger tasks also creates the foundation for a superior result. Our best creative solutions rarely arrive during the stress of the last minute. Once a problem-solving task has begun, the brain continues to work on solutions in its subconscious. The longer we leave between starting on the problem and finishing it, the more opportunity both our conscious *and* subconscious have to work on finding the best, most creative solutions.

6. **Schedule some time for fun.** A balanced life is a combination of work, rest and play. Sometimes procrastination is a sign we are stressed and need an outlet. Dr Neil Fiore, in *The Now Habit (2007),* recommends scheduling time each week for guilt-free leisure activities to lower stress, refresh our energy and attitude and beat procrastination.

7. **Think about the negative consequences of not doing it.** If the goal itself doesn't motivate you enough to move into action, then perhaps the consequences of *not* taking action are motivation enough. For example, you find yourself in 'analysis paralysis', struggling to perfect a presentation. Another hour won't add any substantive extra value, nor will it allay your fears about how you and your presentation will be received; however, the extra hour you take *will* have negative consequences on other people: packaging the rest of the meeting papers will be delayed awaiting your 'perfect' presentation; the meeting attendees will receive the documents late; and you risk being perceived as someone who is inconsiderate of others and disorganised, not a team player and who cannot be trusted to deliver on time.

8. **Work towards being a 'no excuses' person.** Have an honest conversation with a trusted friend, accountability partner, work colleague or coach and examine your best procrastination excuses that are obstacles preventing you from making prog-

ress in relation to your highest goals. Those excuses may be of your own doing or they may involve something or someone external to you. You uncovered many of these excuses when analysing your 'obstacles' in the *Personal Accountability Code*™ SPOT analysis exercise. Brainstorm a series of activities that will either eliminate or mitigate each excuse and schedule these activities into a concrete plan of action.

9. **Break the obsessive-compulsive email habit.** Don't read your email and get caught up in someone else's priorities before you have prioritised your own goals first. The same applies to your social networks, newsfeeds and other automated email messages that flood your inbox. Take more control of your inbox by turning off your email notifications.

10. **Improve your skills.** Your procrastination may simply be a direct result of not having the right skill set to deal with the task, so you don't know how to approach it. Once you accept that this is the situation, decide on one of three options: learn what you need to complete the task; delete it from your task list; or delegate it to someone else who does have the required skill.

6. How to Focus on Goals When ____ Gets in the Way

Sometimes life gets in the way of the goals we set for ourselves. It might be unplanned work, family or health issues that require your attention. From time to time, that's okay. It's important that we are flexible enough to work around changing priorities if the need arises.

Other things get in the way of our focusing on our goals—things that are more our own doing:

- Procrastinating due to unresolved fear and personal productivity issues. (*If procrastination rings true for you, review the '10 Tips of Overcoming Procrastination'.*)
- Having too many goals and priorities competing for your attention. Unless you take specific action to narrow your selections and commit only your highest goals to the top of the priority list (*and give up something in return*), they will never get the attention they deserve.

The *Personal Accountability Code*™ is specifically designed to guide you end-to-end through the goal-achievement process and to keep you focused. Having goals that are aligned with your highest intentions and prioritised and executed with implementation plans is an important foundation for goal focus. However, the best plans are incomplete without a sustainable system of accountability that is unique to you and ensures you are following through on what you said you would do.

To-do lists are not particularly effective when you are faced with real-time decisions for sorting out new priorities on the run. It is all too easy to justify changing around your to-do list if you have no one else to be accountable to. Automated reminders or diary entries are potentially as ineffective for similar reasons. By contrast, accountability partnerships and coaches can work extremely well to help you stay focused when life appears to gets in the way. The specific technique of arranging for someone to call you and have you answer your own list of pre-prepared daily questions can be used as a reminder to keep your daily attention focused and accountable to the goals you have specified as your highest priorities.

For more answers to your most common dilemmas surrounding goal achievement and personal accountability, visit:

www.theaccountabilitycode.com/theaccountabilitycoach

Appendix 1

Do's and Don'ts of Winning with The Personal Accountability Code™

Common derailers of successful goal achievement and what to do about them

Winning with Accountability	Don'ts	Dos
Step 6: How will you stay on track?	Leave goal achievement to chance.	Embrace the winning strategies of SMART+ER goal achievement.
	Procrastinate.	Put an accountability tracking system in place that works for you.
	Go it alone.	Enrol a coach and/or accountability partners.
	Resent or judge or argue with the feedback of an accountability partner.	Be thankful for the input of an accountability partner.
	Obsess about the end game Interpret success or failure solely by the final milestone.	Celebrate the small wins. Celebrate success as the progressive realisation of smaller actions and goals.
	Judge yourself as a complete failure if you miss a deadline or go off course.	Stop berating yourself and be grateful for the learning opportunity and what it can teach you to do differently.
	Give up. Blame others as an excuse to stop or procrastinate in the face of obstacles and setbacks.	Forge Ahead. Accept responsibility for your role in the setback and get on with it.
	Worry about the small stuff.	Focus on the system and process of consistent and steady progress.
	Expect to wake up one day and feel that personal transformation has miraculously occurred on a particular date or milestone event.	Appreciate that personal transformation comes about when you commit to a schedule of regular day-to-day activities that ultimately change what you believe about yourself.

The **Personal** Accountability Code

Winning with Accountability	Don'ts	Dos
Step 5: *How are you getting there?*	Over-engineer the perfect plan. Blinker your assessment of potential goals to just costs or just benefits. Try to over-commit and change everything at once. Commit goals to memory. Keep goals to yourself. Record goals in the future tense as 'I will'.	Take one step TODAY. Take a balanced view of the costs and benefits of your goals. Structure your goal selections to the highest priority using the SMART goal-setting process. Write goals down. Share them with others. Record goals in the positive present tense as 'I am' or 'I have'.
Step 4: *Where are you now?*	Blindly head off down the path of goal selection without taking stock of your SPOT Analysis (Strengths, Problems, Opportunities and Threats).	Make a realistic assessment of your current status and make a plan to: • leverage your personal strengths; • grab opportunities that are crossing your path; • mitigate your personal weaknesses; • address the external threats to your intentions.
Step 3: *Who are you?*	Assume you know everything about yourself. Focus all your efforts on overcoming your problems or weaknesses.	Ask for feedback from others on your strengths and what you could do better. Continue to focus a measured proportion of energy and attention on developing your natural strengths and talents.
Step 2. *Where are You Going?*	Blindly pursue someone else's vision. Take the path you think you should take.	Dare to dream. Take the path you really want to take.
Step :1 *Are You Ready for Change?*	Delude yourself that change is easy. Delay or Procrastinate. Blame others for your weaknesses or failures. Turn a blind eye to your skills in holding others to account for delivering on their promises.	Expect to be uncomfortable. Forge Ahead Now. Take responsibility and take action to address your shortcomings. Seek the support of a peer or coach to improve your capacity to hold others to account.

APPENDIX 2

My Accountability Action Plan

My Vision & Values Statement:

Dimension	Smart Goal	Milestone	Action Step	Reality Check Y/N	Action Step Time Frame
1	1	1	1 2 3 4 5 6 7 8 9 10		- - - - - - - - - -
	2	2	1 2 3 4 5 6 7 8 9 10		- - - - - - - - - -
	3	3	1 2 3 4 5 6 7 8 9 10		- - - - - - - -

My Accountability Action Plan

My Vision & Values Statement:

Dimension	Smart Goal	Milestone	Action Step	Reality Check Y/N	Action Step Time Frame
2	1	1	1 2 3 4 5 6 7 8 9 10		- - - - - - - - - -
	2	2	1 2 3 4 5 6 7 8 9 10		- - - - - - - - - -
	3	3	1 2 3 4 5 6 7 8 9 10		- - - - - - - - -

My Accountability Action Plan

My Vision & Values Statement:

Dimension	Smart Goal	Milestone	Action Step	Reality Check Y/N	Action Step Time Frame
3	1	1	1 2 3 4 5 6 7 8 9 10		- - - - - - - - - -
	2	2	1 2 3 4 5 6 7 8 9 10		- - - - - - - - - -
	3	3	1 2 3 4 5 6 7 8 9 10		- - - - - - - -

My Accountability Action Plan

My Vision & Values Statement:

Dimension	Smart Goal	Milestone	Action Step	Reality Check Y/N	Action Step Time Frame
4	1	1	1 2 3 4 5 6 7 8 9 10		- - - - - - - - - -
	2	2	1 2 3 4 5 6 7 8 9 10		- - - - - - - - - -
	3	3	1 2 3 4 5 6 7 8 9 10		- - - - - - - -

My Accountability Action Plan

My Vision & Values Statement:

Dimension	Smart Goal	Milestone	Action Step	Reality Check Y/N	Action Step Time Frame
5	1	1	1 2 3 4 5 6 7 8 9 10		- - - - - - - - - -
	2	2	1 2 3 4 5 6 7 8 9 10		- - - - - - - - - -
	3	3	1 2 3 4 5 6 7 8 9 10		- - - - - - - -

Dimension	Smart Goal	Milestone	Action Step	Reality Check Y/N	Action Step Time Frame

Di Worrall

Executive Coach

Di's coaching centres on 'accountability that starts at the top'. She knows that, as executives effectively hold themselves, their organisations and people accountable, measurable value is imbued by their leadership. Di's fresh approach to accountability liberates successful leaders to attain sustainable professional and business transformation.

Using empathy and her keen sense of humour, Di generates a safe, positive environment for leaders to achieve greater awareness of and proficiency in their natural motivation, energy and talent. She helps executives hone and increase ways of modelling high performance and leadership accountability.

Di's established track record of success, particularly with business transformation, organisational change and human resources strategy, makes Di invaluable as a top executive coach.

Business Transformation and Change Consulting

With more than 25 years' executive and consulting experience in the public and private sectors, Di understands the issues facing large organisations operating in a multinational business environment. She has walked the same paths and understands the pressures facing high-potential leaders.

For The United Group, Di led the Group Human Resources function, creating a new operating model and strategic planning process. She oversaw the Human Resources due diligence on two major acquisitions, which successfully added 5000 staff to the business, contributing to over 100% increase in share value. Consulting to shared-services provider NSW Businesslink, she led the program to design and implement a best-practice organisational structure, operating model and strategic framework to position the organisation at the leading edge of their market. This program won Di and NSW Businesslink first place in the best 'Customer-Focused Business Model' category of the iCMG Global Architecture Excellence Awards (2012)[4].

Publications

A bestselling author, Di has published numerous books and writes a blog for global leaders of business transformation. Marshall Goldsmith, *NYT* million-selling author of *What Got You Here Won't Get You There* and *MOJO*, commended her 'clarity, simplicity and candour' in a review of Di's #1 Amazon Bestseller *Accountability Leadership: How Great Leaders Build a High-Performance Culture of Accountability and Responsibility*. This seminal work—the first in *The Accountability Code*™ series, transforms perceptions about workplace accountability from punitive to liberating, reinforcing Di as a leading voice in organisational change.

---

[4] ICMG Architecture Awards:
http://www.icmgworld.com/corp/ArchitectureAwards/2012/architecture_awards.asp

Qualifications & Accreditations

Di holds a Graduate Certificate in Change Management from the Australian Graduate School of Management (AGSM), a Graduate Diploma in Tourism from the University of Technology—Sydney (UTS), and a Professional Development Certificate from the Institute of Coaching & Consulting Psychology. Di earned her Bachelor of Business in Human Resources and Industrial Relations from UTS (formerly Nepean CAE). An acclaimed international executive coach, Di holds numerous certifications and accreditations from recognised worldwide organisations, some of which include:

- Certified Coach by Marshall Goldsmith Stakeholder-Centered Coaching
- Certified Graduate of the Australian Institute of Company Directors

OTHER BOOKS FROM DI WORRALL

5 out of 5 stars for

Accountability Leadership—How great leaders build a high-performance culture of accountability and responsibility

The # 1 Amazon bestseller

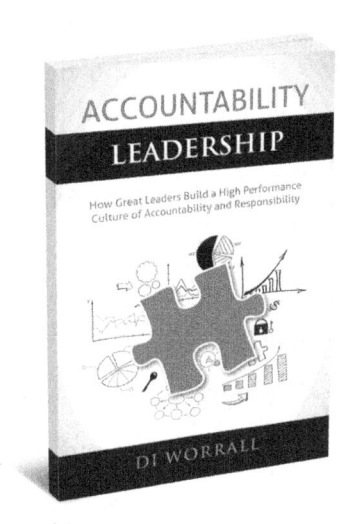

**Still hoping your employees will follow through?
Be certain with the *new* science of accountability**

Great business leaders understand that acceptance of greater accountability and responsibility places individuals, teams, and entire organisations firmly back on the path to success.

But with the evolving nature of 21st-century business, economics, and the growing sector of misunderstood knowledge workers, the practical steps that go into creating a culture of accountability have become more muddled than ever.

Many organisations have seen temporary improvements, implementing traditional systems of accountability in an attempt to drive high performance in the workplace—only to quickly revert back to their old ways, or worse.

The #1 Amazon Bestseller *Accountability Leadership* Will Teach You:

- What it really takes to lead a modern high-accountability organisation
- Why so many of today's employees avoid accountability like the plague, and how to reverse that trend
- Where to find real-world examples of accountability that *work*
- How to create a *sustainable* culture of high accountability and responsibility
- What an accountability plan is, how to create one, and why it's considered the 'secret weapon' behind successful business transformation and change

Filled with down-to-earth case studies and straightforward, easy-to-digest research, *Accountability Leadership* offers practical solutions that are direct, engaging, fast, cost-effective, proven, and easy to implement...

Immediate, Concrete Solutions You'll Take Away From This Book Include:

- How to transform the 'dark side' of accountability into a positive force for change
- Why carrots and sticks no longer work—and what they've been replaced with
- How to create compelling consequences that inspire people to perform at their best, and achieve the ultra-productive work state known as 'flow'
- How to sustain great performance indefinitely through inspiring feedback, feed-forward and follow-through
- How to crack the code of high-accountability conversations, turning confrontation into a productive and positive opportunity

Accountability Leadership Also Sheds Light On Topics Such As...

- How negativity bias covertly sabotages your feedback loop with your employees
- The optimal ratio for positive to negative comments in feedback
- The right amount of autonomy to give employees—without overdoing it
- What lack of recognition is really doing to your workforce *(Clue: it's staggering)*
- The surprising biochemical effect of praise, and why it cannot fail

5 out of 5 stars for Accountability Leadership—Testimonials

'In five jam-packed chapters, and with clarity, simplicity and candour, Worrall teaches corporate leaders how to create a culture of accountability within their organisations. She also reminds us of the often disastrous consequences of failing to do so.'

Marshall Goldsmith—million-selling author of the New York Times bestsellers MOJO and What Got You Here Won't Get You There

'Without accountability, organisations fail. In my experience, you must promote a culture of top-down accountability if you want to promote excellence in your organisation. And that's exactly what this book will teach you how to do. Kudos to the author for choosing to address this oft-neglected issue with a powerful and informative book on accountability leadership.'

Michael Massie—Amazon bestselling author

'Accountability Leadership is a quality resource that will help leaders build a high-performance culture where people achieve because they feel intrinsically accountable. I love how Accountability Leadership has brought together a range of disciplines—including psychology, sociology, and management—to focus leaders on motivating people to feel accountable... and how everyone in an organisation can benefit from this proven and fresh approach.'

Joanna Clark, Business Executive

Accountability Leadership is available from Amazon.com:
http://amzn.com/0992319307

Made in the USA
Monee, IL
12 May 2021